SOCIAL AND EDUCATIONAL ISSUES IN BILINGUALISM AND BICULTURALISM

Edited by

Robert St. Clair
Guadalupe Valdés
Jacob Ornstein-Galicia

UNIVERSITY
PRESS OF
AMERICA

Library of Congress Catalog Card Number: **80-5700**

ACKNOWLEDGMENTS

The emergence of a publication is the result of numerous forces which emanate from various sources and lead into different directions. One of the dominant trends in this regard has been the nature of bilingual education in the Southwest. This is particularly true of the work being done at the University of Texas at El Paso under the leadership of Jacob Ornstein-Galicia and the work being done at New Mexico State University by Guadalupe Valdes. Their respective institutions have played a major role in the creation of this volume through their funding of bilingual research and the sponsoring of regional and national conferences. Another force in the emergence of this volume comes from the Pacific Northwest and the work there done by Robert St. Clair in the area of bilingual literacy and language renewal. This aspect of language planning is more intrinsically related to the political sociology of language, and gratitude must be expressed to many of the Sahaptian Indian River Tribes for their struggle in the creation of bilingual programs.

Special acknowledgment should also be given to the various members of the Office of Academic Publications. Under the directorship of Betty Ash, they have greatly assisted in processing this volume. One who has been most instrumental in the editorial process has been Sharon Mills. Through her efforts, this volume has finally emerged into print. She has spent countless hours reworking the format and redeveloping the final copy of the volume.

The Academic Publications Office at the University of Louisville and the research centers at the University of Texas at El Paso and at New Mexico State University have provided the much needed support for our work in bilingual and bicultural education. However, many of the social and political forces which led to the creation of this volume are not characteristically associated with such institutions. These forces are the parents and other members of various bilingual communities who have voiced their interest in creating a spontaneous language program in bilingual literacy in their area. This is particularly true of the work done in the Pacific Northwest by the Advocates for Indian Education under the Affiliated tribes of Northwest Indians. This astute group of

v

minority leaders has shared with us their hopes and fears and has made us aware of the seriousness of their plight. They have singled out many of the issues which we attempt to deal with in this volume.

Finally, a similar acknowledgment must come from the various minority communities in the Southwest in which parent groups have voiced their concerns for the bicultural enrichment of their children. These Chicano groups share in many of the dreams expressed by those in the Northwest. Their common quest is for a world of cultural pluralism; and, their common fear is the realization that the host society in which they live does not share in these goals politically, economically, and culturally. Hence, the issues that they raise are commonly shared. These are also the issues that we have come to share. The minority forces in these communities have deeply influenced our research goals. We are pleased to acknowledge their many contributions to this volume.

The Editors

TABLE OF CONTENTS

Part Two: PROBLEMS OF LANGUAGE EDUCATION

x

CHAPTER 1

ON DEFINING SOCIAL AND EDUCATIONAL ISSUES IN

BILINGUAL AND BICULTURAL EDUCATION: AN INTRODUCTORY ESSAY

Robert St. Clair (University of Louisville)
Guadalupe Valdés (New Mexico State University)
Jacob Ornstein-Galicia (University of Texas at El Paso)

In political science, agenda-setting is employed as a basic strategy through which the status-quo is maintained and enforced. This is done by keeping the more volatile and sub-stantive issues of power and control hidden from social scru-tiny and replacing them with a plethora of pseudo-issues for public discussion and debate (Schuman, 1977: 102). This concept is an important one and its relevance is not limited to the discipline of political science. It also plays a role in the study of bilingual and bicultural education where dif-ferent academic and civic traditions co-exist and where a va-riety of perspectives define social and educational issues from a range of conflicting priorities.

The linguist, for example, has been trained to view lan-guage as a formal system of verbal structures. Some of these components relate to the sounds of language and their pat-terns of behavior (phonology), and others are concerned with the internal arrangements of words (morphology) or the linear ordering of these elements within a sentence (syntax). Hence, it is not surprising that when they provide the agenda for research, they tend to focus on linguistic forms and their arrangements within a closed system (Hernandez-Chavez, Cohen, and Beltrano, 1975).

For the administrator of a bilingual program, problems and issues are defined on very different terms. In this case, the focus is on the nature of program practices and staff development (Cordasco, 1976: Part IV), the effects of bilingual education in empirical terms (Zapport and Cruz, 1977), oral proficiency and language dominance (Silverman, Noa and Russell, 1976), the socio-historical foundations of bilingual programs (von Maltitz, 1975) or other forms of tabulating the flow of events within the operation of a program.

Sometimes these approaches develop and provide a perspective which is interdisciplinary in nature. This is evident, for example, in the sociolinguistic approach of Andrew Cohen (1975), the political approach of Murguía (1976), Garcia and de la Garza (1977), Castro (1974), Rosaldo, Seligman and Calvert (1974), Garcia (1974) or Rodríguez (1977). It is this multifactoral and multidimensional understanding of language and education across cultures, however, which continues to provide a more realistic framework for coping with the problems and the issues which one characteristically associates with the field of bilingual and bicultural education. This fact can be readily ascertained in the works of Acuña (1972), Webster (1972), Troike and Modiano (1975) and Simões (1976).

In each of these perspectives on language and the bilingual context, there are theoretical and methodological priorities which define the scope of discussion, delimit alternative approaches, and assign a hierarchy of values to the factual content under evaluation. An understanding of these variations and how they specify the definition of problems and the assignment of issues requires an integration of knowledge which transcends the parameters of any one discipline. It requires a theory of epistemology (Berger and Luckmann, 1966), a philosophy of science (Kuhn, 1970), a view of social history (Forbes, 1973; Moquin, 1972; Matthiessen, 1973; Rendon, 1971; and McWilliams, 1968), a concept of social values (Horkheimer, 1968; Horkheimer and Adorno, 1969), and a theory of social change (Klapp, 1978; and Mueller, 1973).

According to the philosophy of science (Kuhn, 1970), problems originate from anomalies within the theoretical models in use. Thomas Kuhn has developed a structural model of scientific enlightenment which is characterized by three stages in a never ending spiral of progress. The first stage is called normal science and represents a highly stable social fabric in which conflict is nearly non-existent and scientists experience a euphoria which they attribute to having solved the major issues of the day. This golden age is steeped in ritual and reaffirms its existence by glorying in past accomplishments. But, this feeling of euphoria is

an ephemeral one.   With the passage of time, anomalies begin
to occur.   Some definitions appear contradictory, some experiments fail to work, and suspicions begin to emerge about the
infalibility of the model.   This mounting pattern of failure
and suspicion leads to the second stage in the structure of
science, the period of crises.   It is here that values are
questioned and a prevailing spirit of exploration occurs.   As
Kuhn has noted, this period is characterized by a host of
competing models and a search for new insights to old problems.   As these models compete, one is bound to emerge vic-
torious and it is during this time that the third stage of
progression occurs, the period of scientific revolution.   It
is a time when the scientific community is imbued with a
spirit of accomplishment and cognitive growth.   During this
stage of the eternal spiral of progress, there is a flurry of
research in which the older model of the normal science paradigm is re-evaluated and redefined within the theoretical
framework of the new model.   Subsequently, however, the
flurry of activity subsides and the model of revolutionary
science assumes the role of the new normal science within the
scientific community.

What role does this model play within bilingual and bicultural education and how does it defines what problems are
or how issues arise?   For an answer to this question, one
must view each discipline separately.   In the formal study of
language, for example, linguists have witnessed a change from
the normal science of Leonard Bloomfield (1933) and his students to the revolutionary science model of Noam Chomsky
(1957; 1965).   Hence, those who are working in the bilingual
and bicultural context will usually reflect the research paradigm that they were trained in.   As for the foundations of
language education, there has also been a change in theoretical priorities.   Under the normal science model of Lawrence
Cremin (1964; 1965) the school provides for social mobility
and it is this characteristic which marks the American school
system as being unique.   However, as Collin Greer (1973;
1974) the claims of social mobility through education are
grossly overstated.   The school system has been used in the
training of the urban working class (Violas, 1978) and as a
sorting machine for technocracy and industry (Spring, 1976),
or an expression of internal colonialism (Iverson, 1978).   It
is for these reasons, among others, that Ivan Illich (1972)
has addressed the issue of deschooling society or Paulo
Freire (1974) has concerned himself the pedagogy of the

oppressed or Barry Schwartz (1972) has asked for affirmative education. Whether these non-traditional models of education are in a critical phase or in a revolutionary one is for the historiographer of the foundations of education. However, the significance differences among these groups will be reflected in just what they are willing to consider problems or construe as issues.

The model espoused by Thomas Kuhn (1970) lacks in its ability to account for social change within the matrix of the complex industrial society with its fragmented interest groups and feelings of alienation (Berger, Berger, and Kellner, 1974). His model can only account for the more homogenous scientific communities in which the agenda for social interaction is severely limited to the research interests of the ruling paradigm. Hence, a more instructive approach to social change and conflicts of values can be found in the information theory model of Orrin Klapp (1978).

In information theory, the channel carries the code and provides the link between the speaker and the hearer. This is accomplished, in part, by the process of encoding the message at one end and decoding it at the other. What Orrin Klapp provides in his extension of this model is the process of selectivity. He argues, for example, that a person may scan the code at times for more information or close the channel at other times when the incoming information proves to be too adverse or disconcerting. He refers to this latter condition as "social noise." Noise is anything coming in a channel that interferes with signals that one is trying to receive. But, there are times when signals themselves turn out to be social noise. This occurs when the message is ambiguous (semantic noise) or when it is incompatible with the social expectations of the hearer (stylistic noise) or when a perfectly good signal is irrelevant, redundant or produces a sheer overload of information (cognitive clutter) or when the incoming signal is the basis for cognitive dissonance (contagious noise). As Orrin Klapp notes,

> "Noise ... defined relative to receivers'
> needs not senders' intentions (To those
> seeking beauty, ugliness is noise; to
> those seeking harmony, discord is noise;
> to those who want neatness, clutter is

4

noise; to those concerned about their
souls, sin is noise).

(Orrin Klapp, 1978:5)

When the metaphor of the communication channel and the
selectivity of the hearer is extended to account for social
interaction, it leads to an informative discussion of open
and closed societies. The open society has always been defined in the literature in positive terms (Popper, 1952). It
has been described as the society in which there is always a
free flow of information and in which multiple life styles
co-exist. In this sense, the open society is similar to the
model of cultural pluralism which Kallen (1924) proposed over
a half-century ago. The same underlying values can be found
in literature about the need for an open mind (Rokeach,
1960). It is a mind that is open to information and which
always desires to know and understand the nature of change
and social conflict. Orrin Klapp (1978; 12) challenges these
assumptions. He notes that there are several times when too
much newness leads to confusion and social noise. This, in
part, is what Alvin Toffler (1970) spoke about in his discussion of future shock; and, this is what James G. Miller
(1960; 1971) has referred to in the literature as information
overload. Under such circumstances, perfectly good information is capable of becoming noise and interferes with getting
the information that one needs. It leaves one struggling in
a sea of exogenous signals without a set of values by which
to evaluate them or a tradition with which to filter them and
test them for truth, goodness, or value. This barrage of new
data creates a stress situation and requires a greater effort
in integrating new concepts into the existing framework of
knowledge and experience; it creates a state of cognitive
dissonance (Festinger, 1957:3) which necessitates an avoid-
ance reaction or an attenuation of the incoming signal; it
also leads to affective dissonance. As might be expected, a
classic defensive strategy against information overload is
selective perception. This takes the form of specialization
of work in which a shield is developed to restrict what one
must know to a narrow sphere of experience and professional
expertise (Bledstein, 1976), and this in itself leads to a
sense of alienation and despair (Schacht, 1970).

5

As Alvin Toffler (1970) noted in his discussion of information overload in a complex industrial society, too much information can lead to decision lags. But, the problem does not end there. There are also lags in consensus between scientific research and the scholars who fail to keep up with the pace; and, there are lags in decision making among administrators and bureaucrats who fail to use theoretical information effectively even when it is available to them; and, there are also lags in consensus in the domain of public opinion where the populace remains uninformed and apathetic to the very issues which influence their lives. The implications of this research on information overload for the study of social and educational issues in bilingualism can be readily ascertained. An informative example can be found in the area of lexicography and merits elucidation here. The lexicographer's task is the establishment of entries into a dictionary. In some countries, the dictionary includes detailed citations of great moments in the literature of the nation. This elitist view of the lexicon still exists and can be found in its most lucid form in the Oxford English Dictionary. The normal trend, however, has been to cite words, give their etymological background, provide a key to pronunciation, and classify the forms in accordance with the parts of speech. During the 1930's linguists reacted to the elitist and prescriptivist practices of language educators and proposed that the dictionary should not exclude other forms of English. What they had proposed become a reality in the late 1950s when the Webster's Third International Dictionary appeared with citations of dialectal forms and slang words. However, at this time, the theory which espoused such a view was no longer in acceptance as the scientific community had undergone a scientific revolution. Hence, there was a tremendous lag in information and its application in the public domain. The public reacted negatively as it based its decision on the lexicographical practices which were espoused prior to the turn of the century. The linguists reacted negatively because they viewed the change from the perspective of the more recent theoretical framework of transformational grammar. And, as for the dictionary, it remains an anomaly in time and space. Obviously, each of these groups viewed the dictionary from their own traditions. The lexicographers who created the dictionary did not envisage any problems or issues. It reflected their structuralist thinking. The consensus lag on behalf of the public, however, did create a stir as it saw the lexicon as a problem which generated a host of issues. On the other extreme of the consensus lag was the neo-structuralist who came armed with different views and saw the dictionary as a different problem with different issues.

Orrin Klapp (1978) argues that when a society is in need of change and experiences media hunger, it opens up its selectivity and searches for new information and insights. This state of social action is comparable to the period of crises in Thomas Kuhn's (1970) theory of scientific revolutions. However, when a society reaches a stage of information overload, it tends to close out exogenous signals and seek refuge in a reminiscience of the past where the information is more readily comprehensible. Hence, society oscillates between openings and closings and these may be viewed as either being good or bad.

	Closing	Opening
Good	Gain: Emphasis on the norm	Gain: Emphasis on new information
Bad	Loss: Overstressing of traditional boundaries	Loss: Transgression of tradition

Bad Openings:	folly, crime, lawlessness, waste, error, vulgar, tasteless, disloyal, interbreeding...
Good Openings:	open-minded, tolerant, receptive, omnivorous, inquisitive, experimental, permissive...
Bad Closing:	censorship, puritan, intolerant, arrogant, provincial, narrowminded, dogmatic, ignorant...

7

Good Closing: loyalty, self-control, prudence, morality, selective, discreet, cautious, antiseptic...

In the game of life, Orrin Klapp (1978:20) notes, there are oscillations between variety and redundancy as well as a search for information or a return to chaos or entropy. At these times, society becomes selected to either indigenous signals which are familiar, high in redundancy, local in reference, trusted, and sacred, or exogenous signals which are strange in origin, outside of one's direct experience, requiring a redefinition of the situation, and profane. This dichotomy is reminiscent of the one made by Ferdinand Tönnies (1957) between Gemeinschaft and Gesellschaft and by Mircea Eliade (1959) between the sacred and the profane.

Indigenous Signals	Exogenous Signals
Gemeinschaft (community)	Gesellschaft (society)
Sacred	Profane
Closed	Open

When a community is threatened, it reaffirms its values and tends to avoid that which is strange, unknown, or foreign to its way of life. It selects for indigenous signals and excludes the exogenous ones. Similarly, when one is surfeited by tradition and ritual, there is a hunger for newness and under such circumstances the society opens up and seeks exogenous signals while attenuating those which remain indigenous.

8

```
                        INFORMATION
                            |
                            |
                            |
        Discovery           |        Ritual
        Growth              |        Tradition
        Liberal             |        Conservative
                            |
                            |
                            |
VARIETY - - - - - - - - - - + - - - - - - - - - REDUNDANCY
                            |
                            |
                            |
                            |
        Information         |        Banality
         overload           |        Boredom
        Social Noise        |
                            |
                            |
                            |
                        ENTROPY
                        (disorder)
```

When one seeks new information, the channels of communication are open to signals rather than to noise.   These signals may be exogenous as in times of growth and discovery or
indigenous as in times of tradition and conservativism.   The
transition from redundancy to variety cuts across another
axis.   If the signals are redundant and reinforcing (indigenous) they provide a sense of community.   But, when these
signals become banal and overly-redundant, they lead to entropy and chaos.   Similarly, the openness and excitement of
variety may also turn into social noise as in the case of information overload, and this results in a state of disorder
and confusion.   What this means, in essence, is that social
groups oscillate between openings and closings depending on
whether or not they perceive their lives as being in a state
of disorder or bombarded by change.   In order to understand
where a group or an individual is coming from in the oscillations of social change, one must ascertain where that group
or individual has been.   Hence, the relevance of social

9

```
                        INFORMATION
                            |
                            |
                            |
   Good Opening             |        Good Closing
     search                 |          nostalgia
     innovation             |          ritual
                            |
                            |
VARIETY - - - - - - - - - -|- - - - - - - - REDUNDANCY
                            |
                            |
                            |
   Bad Opening              |        Bad Closing
     clutter                |          boredom
                            |          meaningless
                            |
                            |
                            |
                         ENTROPY
```

history can be found in reconstructing one's biographical history and the root metaphors of one's culture as these maps of reality soon become plans for social action and public behavior.

In order to understand how one group is threatened by some values while other groups are not, it is necessary to first consider how social reality is constructed. According to Peter Berger and Thomas Luckmann (1966), social reality is not only constructed, it is socially distributed. Each person has a different biographical history and approaches adult hood with different coping strategies and personal experiences. What they have come to learn may or may not be known to others. The world of the auto mechanic is not known or shared with many who drive automobiles to and from their way to work. Similarly, the abstract concerns of the professional philosopher are not within the scope and interest of many who remain ignorant of the literature in that field. More importantly, the professional politician who creates and develops legislation on bilingual and bicultural education, may not even be remotely aware of the social worlds inhabited by the children of the barrio for whom the laws were supposedly written and enacted.

If people live in a world in which they have constructed a repertoire of social realities, how is intersubjectivity possible? How can the teacher who does not live in a Chicano community and does not share its language and culture come to understand the children in his or her classroom? There are, apparently, two traditional approaches to these questions. From the point of view of the positivist (Comte, 1969), people come to understand one another (intersubjectivity) because they live in the same physical surroundings and see the same things. When misunderstandings occur, it is argued, it is because our instruments for detecting the physical world are not sophisticated enough, but eventually this problem will be solved through the advance of science. The opposing view of epistemology, can be found in the sociology of knowledge and particularly in the writings of Peter Berger and Charles Luckmann (1966). They agree with Kant (1956) that one may never know what the physical universe is like (noumena) because one is limited in vision and hearing to the world of impressions and appearances (phenomena). Furthermore, along with these physical and physiological constraints on knowing and understanding, there are cultural influences. Not only do people from different cultures come to have contrasting interpetations of social behavior, but within any one culture there exist a repertoire of social realities within every person. Hence, knowledge is socially constructed and highly contextualized so that people who have different experiences and different avenues of access within a society, exist in different social worlds and possess different views of knowledge. When people do share a sense of community, it is because they share the same expectations and beliefs and have been socialized along similar lines.

Since people undergo different patterns of socialization, it can be readily seen that the child who is born into the tradition of the power elite (Mills, 1956) has a different bibliographical history from the child who is raised in the barrio (Forbes, 1973). The former is born into a tradition of power and wealth and is sent to the finest prep schools or boarding schools, is guaranteed a college education, a law degree at one of the Ivy League schools and a protected position within one of the multi-national conglomerates. The latter, by way of contrast, is born into

11

poverty and will remain powerless within the system which has oppressed his or her parents. This child is not guaranteed any formal schooling of any quality and will suffer a life time of alienation and neglect. They are on different time tracks (Lyman and Scott, 1970: 191). They hold different social expectations, and they define themselves in highly disparate terms. They have different constructions of social reality and they do not share the same forms of knowledge or education. Hence, when they become adults, their views of social problems and issues will differ greatly. The former will see bilingual education in terms of control through the common medium of English, while the latter will see it as an attempt to degrade and devalue their own mother tongue, Spanish.

These different perspectives on the agenda of life raise the fundamental question of who sets the agenda and for whom is it meant to benefit. For the administrator of a bilingual program, these questions may be short-circuited by a concern for complying with the law and its intent. The task becomes one of professional efficiency. However, from the point of view of the critical theorist (Horkheimer, 1968), the prior question is one of who sets the agenda. Who has defined the problems and designated the nature of the issues to be discussed? Within their framework, the teacher should not be merely an enforcer of the system, but a social agent. Obviously, each of these models of the bilingual teacher creates a different set of definitions of just what constitutes a problem and how issues are to be defined. Consequently, these questions need to be reiterated when reading the following collection of essays on social and educational issues in bilingual education.

Jorge Guitart (Chapter Two) discusses the question of language loyalty and notes how it develops when the language of a group is threatened and its speakers react with an awakened sentiment to save their endangered language. This threat may come from the purist who views the addition of foreign words into his lexicon as a time for retrenchment against change, or it may come from the speaker of an ethnic minority who witnesses the gradual demise of his or her native speech in the politics of accommodation where the agenda for public commerce is done in English, the mainstream language. Guitart offers some insightful distinctions between ethnic loyalty and language loyalty. He notes that the melting pot model, which he renames the Anglo-American Assimilation Pot, is the driving force behind the loss of an ethnic tongue. But, the shift in language does not entail a shift in ethnicity and the quest for ethnic loyalty. In discussing how the conventional educational system attempts to deal with students who are monolingual in their ethnic tongue or bilingual, he notes that they are ill prepared to handle the situation within the current curriculum. Furthermore, he raises the issue of Standard Spanish and questions its validity and legitimation within a multi-ethnic and multi-cultural context where its usage continues to go unquestioned. The social and educational issues, in this case, are in need of reassessment. It appears that the language education programs in the United States, for example, have confused ethnic loyalty with language loyalty.

Guadalupe Valdes-(Chapter Three) addresses the problem of language development and its conflict with the teaching of the standard language. In her research, she has commented on the interesting but not uncommon situation in which Mexican-American students are assumed to be competent in Spanish, but turn out to be English dominant. They have difficulty in teaching the language, communicate only superficially, have difficulty in reading, encounter problems in spelling, and are intimidated by the mere attempt of conversing in the language. The double-bind comes from the administration of the program in which they are not allowed to compete with beginning students of Spanish and are forced to enroll in a course on Spanish for native speakers. Obviously, the social and educational problems in this situation have been defined rather differently by each of these group. The courses themselves are designed to teach grammar, but it is questioned whether or not this motive can even begin to meet the various needs and problems of the students who approach such a course with different set of priorities. Furthermore, there is the problem of the standard dialect and its legitimation over other dialects of the language. In addition, there are the instructional problems relating to the teaching of English-dominant vs Spanish-speaking bilinguals. Each of these problem areas are cast within the perspectives of the school system, and the social expectations that the populace has about Mexican-Americans and their assumed proficiency in Spanish. However, when the students and their rights are taken into consideration, the conflict of values and the nature of the agenda imposed upon them becomes an issue in itself.

Robert St. Clair and James Eiseman (Chapter Four) discuss the process of political socialization and its relationship to the language education of the bilingual child. In
their work, they cite how a tradition of language education
has been characteristically associated with colonialism and
how the school curriculum became the forum for the implementation of socializing models in which the power structure was
portrayed as heroes and those who were oppressed and controlled were depicted in villainous terms. In addition, they
also note how power is used to legitimize knowledge and pro-
tect the status quo. The implications of this research for
bilingual education are also discussed. These range from the
setting of internal colonialism common to the reservation system and the use of dependency and neo-colonialism among migrants and farm laborers. This research is reminiscent of
the Americanization movement in teaching English as a foreign
language or as a second language to immigrants over the last
century.

Betty Lou Dubois (Chapter Five) looks at the British
tradition of language education and assesses its role in the
classroom setting in American universities. Her discussion
of the topic includes a clarification of the different kinds
of English which have emerged in the United States as exten-
sions of the British influence, the kinds of English used by
foreign students who enter the United States to travel at
American universities, and an evaluation of the English program at her home university in New Mexico. Comparisons are
made with the teaching of Spanish for the Spanish-speaking,
and the special needs of West African students studying in
the United States. What is significant about this study is
that it provides an insightful comparison between two dominant traditions in the Southwest: the teaching of English
and Spanish. Such a comparison highlights certain similarities which are common to both languages and puts them into a
common perspective. viz., language education and information
processing.

In Chapter Six, Anthony Lozano discusses the kinds of
problems involved in teaching a standard dialect to Chicano
students who are studying abroad. His work involves a program at the University of Vera Cruz in Jalapa, Mexico. In
that city, Chicano students are faced with standard Spanish,

14

Chicano Spanish, and the elementary or near-standard Spanish spoken by the Ango students. The policy for resolving this state of affairs requires the Chicano student to learn standard Spanish as an additional dialect. However, the demonstrated proficiency of such students covered a wide range of abilities from fluency to virtually no Spanish. In addition, there were dialectal differences among these students who did command the language. In considering the three approaches to teaching Spanish to Spanish speakers, he considers the biloquialism or additional dialect approach over the erradication approach or the appreciation of dialect differences format and discusses the various kinds of techniques for accomplishing this. The problems that he encounters have been intrinsically related to the kinds of needs that he perceived in teaching within the framework of bidialectalism. Once again, this points to the need for an in-depth assessment of needs and goals in the language classroom.

Florence Barkin (Chapter Seven) addresses the problem of code switching in Chicano Spanish among the migrant workers in Florida. The alternation, in this case, was between Spanish and English, and the reason for switching ranges in topics chosen, role-relationships, turn-taking, and emphasis. She argues that educators should recognize the difference between Chicanos who do switch from Spanish to English because they are sensitive to the two languages and those who don't. The switch does not necessarily mean that one cannot recall the appropriate Spanish lexical items, but that the choice of lexical items signals a deliberate attempt to convey an additional affective meaning. Hence, what would be a problem in the eyes of some educators is not a problem to the more sophisticated student of language in the classroom. This message is an important one and bears reiteration in inservice courses.

In Chapter Eight, Geraldo Kaprosy and Robert St. Clair present a socio-political analysis of literacy and discuss the order society concept in which language policy is dictated by the interests of a power elite. They also include an explication of labelling theory and characterize the three stages of linguistic oppressions. The moral entrepreneur who incites a ferverent interest around his or her common cause is usually not discussed by administrators of bilingual programs. Neither are the victims of the labelling process.

What appears to be of central concern to those who are involved in the administration or the implementation of bilingual literacy is the process of social enforcement. It is
in this context that the dilemma of the teacher of bicultural
education becomes of one of critical concern. If the teacher
is aware of who is served by such legislation and disagrees
with its intent, that individual can become a social agent.
However, there is a double bind. The teacher also stands the
risk of being misunderstood by the administrator as one who
is inefficient and is working counter to the system. On the
other hand, if the teacher does an efficient job of complying
with the rules, then his or her conscious will be the source
of anxiety and despair. Suggestions are provided for coping
with the problem of bicultural dissonance.

Fritz Hensey (Chapter Nine) focuses on the nature of
language variation in bilingual education and develops a discussion on past practices where the student was judged by a
well-defined norm based on rote behavior and critical of individual creativity. He notes that foreign language texts
fail to define major variations in usage in a pedagogically
useful way, and sees some value in the sociolinguistic approach to such matters of variation. In particular, he emphasizes what has been referred to in the literature as the
dependency hypothesis where disparate dialectal forms of language at the phonetic level are united and causally related
to the same underlying forms at the systematic phonemic
level. The examples that he cites are of a morphosyntactic
nature and relate to the forms of language usages in the
Southwest. The problems that he defines are of a syntagmatic
or linear order and a paradigmatic or hierarchical order. He
offers suggestions for using his approach to language variation in the classroom, but considers it to be more diagnostic in nature and consequently descriptive in format. The
explication of variation provided by Hensey is characteristic
of the normal science paradigm of generative phonology and
offers many insights into certain problems in bilingual education.

Another approach to variables can be found in the work
of Lilith Haynes (Chapter Ten). She notes that social and
linguistic variation occurs in all classrooms and is not
limited to the experience of the bilingual child. Some of
the variables that she addresses are of a macro-societal

nature, teacher variables of knowledge of language and the content areas, and teacher-student variables of familiarity with variation, and acceptability of the perspective of the student. The complexity of sociolinguistic variables is documented and comments are offered with regard to the bilingual classroom. Unlike the previous chapter in which problems were closely defined from the total perspective of only one discipline, the recognition of linguistic variation in this chapter appears to be more open and interdisciplinary in nature. It is the kind of approach that comes from one who has been involved in the context of the classroom and has witnessed the multiplicity of factors which can and do impinge on a child's linguistic behavior. As Haynes notes, variation provides a source of illumination and insight both inside and outside the classroom.

All of these chapters provide different perspectives on the social and educational problems of bilingualism. They include the formal linguistic analyses, the assessment of reading, the nature of variability in theory and in practice, and essays on socio-political approaches to language. From the point of view of society, some of these problems can be seen as a challenge (good openings), or a return to the basics (good closings). However, they can also be viewed as unwanted signals (bad closings) or a return to banality (bad openings). For the ethnic minority that is searching for its roots, for example, there is a sensitivity to the indigenous signals of the past and the sacred values of the group and a closing of the unwanted exogenous signals of the host society which threatens it. For the administrator or the politician who advocates juridicial compliance, the mainstream represents the tradition of sacred values and ritual. Such a person would characterize the minorities' attempt to return to ethnicity as a threat to the host society and would view such pleas to be characteristic of exogenous signals which could lead to either cognitive clutter or banality. Hence, one must view each of these chapters from their own perspectives and derive what problems and issues their own biographical histories, academic training, and personal experiences bring.

REFERENCES

Acuña, Rudolfo. Occupied America: The Chicano Struggle Toward Libernation. N.Y.: Canfield Press, Harper and Row, 1972.

Berger, Peter and Lukmann, Thomas. The Social Construction of Social Reality. N.Y.: Doubleday, 1966.

Berger, Peter; Berger, Brigitte; and Kellner, Hansfried. The Homeless Mind: Modernization and Consciousness. N.Y.: Vintage Press Books, 1974.

Bledstein, Burton J. The Culture of Professionalism: The Middle Class and The Development of Higher Education in America. N.Y.: W. W. Norton, 1916.

Bloomfield, Leonard. Language. N.Y.: Harper and Row, 1933.

Castro, Tony. Chicano Power: The Emergence of Mexican Americans. N.Y.: Saturday Review Press, E. P. Dutton and Co., 1974.

Chomsky, A. Noam. Syntactic Structures. Paris: Mouton and Co., 1957.

Chomsky, A. Noam. Aspects of The Theory of Syntax. Cambridge, Mass.: M.I.T. Press, 1965.

Cohen, Andrew. A Socialinguistic Approach to Bilingual Education: Experiments in the American Southwest. Rowley, Mass.: Newbury House, 1975.

Comte, Auguste. Sociologie: Textes Choisis. Paris France: Presses Universitaires de France, 1969.

Cordasco, Francesco (Ed.). Bilingual Schooling in the United States: A Sourcebook for Educational Personnel. N.Y.: Webster Division, McGraw-Hill Book Co., 1976.

Cremin, Lawrence A. The Transformation of the School: Progressivism in American Education. N.Y.: Vintage Book, 1964.

Cremin, Lawrence A. The Genius of American Education. N.Y.: Vintage, 1965.

Eliade, Mircea. The Sacred and the Profane: The Significance of Religious Myth, Symbolism, and Ritual Within Life and Culture. N.Y.: Harvest Book, 1957.

Festinger, Leon. A Theory of Cognitive Dissonance. Palo Alto, California: Stanford University Press, 1957.

Forbes, Jack D. Aztecas Del Norté: The Chicanos of Aztlán. Greenwich, Conn.: Fawcett Publications, 1973.

Freire, Paulo. Pedagogy of the Oppressed. N.Y.: Seabury Press, 1974.

Garcia, F. Chris. (Ed.). La Causa Politica: A Chicano Political Reader. West Lafayette, Indiana: University of Notre Dame Press, 1974.

Garcia, F. Chris and de la Garza, Rudolph O. The Chicano Political Experience: Three Perspectives. North Scituate, Mass.: Duxbury Press, 1977.

Greer, Collin (Ed.). The Solution as Part of the Problem: Urban Education Reform in the 1960s. N.Y.: Perennial Library, 1973.

Greer, Collin (Ed.). Divided Society: The Ethnic Experience in American. N.Y.: Basic Books, 1974.

Gutierrez, Jose Angel. A Gringo Manual on How to Handle Mexicans. Crystal City, Texas: Wintergarden Publishing House, n.d.

Hernandez-Chavez, Eduardo; Cohen, Andrew; and Beltramo, A. (Eds.) El Lenguaje de Los Chicanos: Regional and Social Characteristics of Language used by Mexican Americans. Arlington, Virginia: Center for Applied Linguistics, 1975.

Horkheimer, Max, Kritische Theorie (Bund I, II). Frankfort am Main: S. Fischer Verlag GmbH, 1969.

19

Horkheimer, Max and Adorno, Theodor W. Dialektik der Auf-klärung. Frankfurt am Main: S. Fischer Verlag GmbH, 1969.

Illich, Ivan. Deschooling Society. N.Y.: Harrow Books, 1972.

Iverson, Katherine. Civilization and Assimilation in the Colonized Schooling of Native Americans. In Philip Alt-bach and Gail Kelly (Eds.). Education and Colonialism. N.Y.: Longman, 1978.

Kallen, H. M. Democracy versus the Melting Pot. In H. M. Kallen (Ed.), Culture and Democracy in the United States. N.Y.: Boni and Liveright, 1924.

Kant, Immanuel. Kritik der reinen Vernunft. Hamburg: Felix Meiner Verlag, 1956.

Klapp, Orrin. Opening and Closing: Strategies of Informa-tion Adaptation in Society. Cambridge: Cambridge Uni-versity Press, 1978.

Kuhn, Thomas S. The Structure of Scientific Revolutions (Re-vised Edition). Chicago: Chicago University Press, 1970.

McWilliams, Carey. North from Mexico: The Spanish Speaking People of the United States. Westport, Conn.: Green-wood Press, 1968.

Matthiessen, Peter. Sal Si Puedes: -Cesar Chavez and the New American Revolution. N.Y.: Dell Publishing, 1973.

Miller, James G. Information Input and Overload. Psycho-pathology. American Journal of Psychiatry, 1960, 16, 695-704.

Miller, James G. Living System: The Group. Behavioral Science, 1971, 16, 277-398.

Mills, C. Wright. Power Elite. Oxford: Oxford University Press, 1956.

Moquin, Wayne. A Documentary History of the Mexican Americans. N.Y.: Bantam Books, 1972.

Mueller, Claus. The Politics of Communications: A Study in The Political Sociology of Lanugage, Socialization and Legitimation. Oxford: Oxford University Press, 1973.

Murguía, Edward. Assimilation, Colonialism and the Mexican-American People. Austin, Texas: Center for American Studies, University of Texas, 1976.

Popper, Karl R. The Open Society and Its enemies (Volumes 1 and 2). London: Routledge and Kegan Paul, 1952.

Rendon, Armando B. Chicano Manifesto: The History and Aspirations of the Second Largest Minority in America. N.Y.: Collier Books, 1971.

Rodríguez, Olga (Ed.). The Politics of Chicano Liberation. N.Y.: Pathfinder Press, 1977.

Rokeach, Milton. The Open and Closed Mind. N.Y.: Basic Books, 1960.

Rosaldo, Renato; Seligmann, Gustav L., and Calvert, Robert A. Chicano: The Beginning of Bronze Power. N.Y.: William Morrow, 1974.

Schacht, Richard. Alienation. N.Y.: Achor Books, 1970.

Schwartz, Barry N. (Ed.). Affirmative Education: Radical Approaches to Education. N.Y.: Spectrum Books, 1972.

Schumann, David. A Preface to Politics. Lexington, Mass.: D. C. Heath and Company, 1977.

Silverman, Robert J., Noa, Joslyn K., and Russell, Randall H. Oral Language Tests For Bilingual Students: an Evaluation of Language Domains and Proficiency Instruments. (Forward by John C. Molina). Portland, Oregon: Northwest Regional Educational Laboratory, 1976.

Simoés, Antónío, Jr. (Ed.). The Bilingual Child: Research and Analysis of Existing Educational Themes. N.Y.: Academic Press, 1976.

Spring, Joel. The Sorting Machine: National Educational Policy Since 1945. N.Y.: David McKay Co., 1976.

Toffler, Alvin. Future Shock N.Y.: Random House, 1970.

Tönnies, Ferdinand. Community and Society (Gemeinschaft und Gesellschaft). N.Y.: Harper Torchbooks, 1957.

Troike, Rudolph C. and Modiano, Nancy. Proceedings of the First International Conference on Bilingual Education. Arlington, Virginia: Center for Applied Linguistics, 1975.

Violas, Paul. The Training of the Urban Working Class: A History of Twentieth Century American Education. Chicago, Illinois: Rand McNally, 1978.

von Maltitz, Frances Willard. Living and Learning in Two Languages: Bilingual-Bicultural Education. N.Y.: McGraw-Hill, 1975.

Webster, Staten W. Knowing and Understanding the Socially Disadvantaged Ethnic Minority Groups. Scranton, Pa.: Intext Educational Publishing, Intext Textbook Co., 1972.

Zappert, Laraine Testa and Cruz, B. Roberto. Bilingual Education: An Appraisal of Empirical Research. Berkeley, California: Bay Area Bilingual Educational League/Lau Center, 1977.

CHAPTER 2

THE QUESTION OF LANGUAGE LOYALTY[1]

Jorge M. Guitart
State University of New York at Buffalo

The term 'language loyalty' was introduced by Weinreich to designate the sentiment awakened in the speakers of an endangered language that will lead them to defend that language. He has defined it as follows:

> a principle--its specific content varies from case to case--in the name of which people will rally themselves and their fellow speakers consciously and explicitly to resist changes in either the functions of their language (as a result of language shift) or in the structure of vocabularly (as a consequence of interference (Weinreich 1968:99).

"One would suspect," writes Weinreich, "that a rudiment of this feeling is natural in every user of the language." (1968:99). The numberous cases of language conflict throughout the ages certainly support this notion. Human experience being inextricably bound with language experience, it is natural that an attack on a language would be interpreted as an attack on its speakers, calling for some response. The intensity of the response will depend on the intensity of the threat, whether real or imagined. It may be very mild, as when a purist laments the use of a foreign word, or it may be very violent, as when speakers take to the streets and even lose their lives over some language issue. Language riots are not frequent but they do occur from time to time. At the time of this writing, mid 1976, deadly violence still rages in Soweto, South Africa, as a result of an official decision to impose Afrikaans as the language of education on Bantu groups.

While in the history of mankind many people have literally give their lives for their language, many others have surrendered theirs without putting up a fight, either in the real or figurative sense of the word. For language loyalty is awakened only when speakers have a positive attitude toward their tongue, which is not always the case. As Weinreich has pointed out, language loyalty is more intense in situations of language contact, but only if the mother tongue is seen both as superior to the encroaching language and as threatened by it. If the other language is perceived as more useful and/or prestigious, 'betrayal' is the norm. When contact is due to immigration, it is normal for the children of immigrants to eventually abandon the language of their parents, even in cases where parents have remained loyal and are actively engaged in the defense of their tongue. In the absence of a strong sense of language loyalty, the parents themselves end up using--however imperfectly--the language of the host (and dominant) culture in their dealings with their own children. The foregoing phenomena are commonplace in the history of immigrant groups in the United States, a country where language maintenance efforts on behalf of non-English tongues in general have not been very successful and where language 'betrayal' has been the norm in situations of language contact.

In 1966 Joshua Fishman and his colleagues published their monumental Language Loyalty in the United States (henceforth referred to as LLUS), where the travails of language-maintenance in the United States are extensively documented. In his integrative review at the end of that volume, Glazer (1966:361) summarized very aptly the fate suffered by non-English languages in the United States:

> Whether it was one of the great international tongues with a vast literature, such as German, Spanish, or French; or a language of peasants with a scanty literature or press, such as Ukrainian; or an exotic and proud language not widely known, such as Hungarian; or a language such as Yiddish, that incorporated in itself a major national and cultural movement--all, it seems, regardless of their position, their history, their strength, the character of the groups that brought them to this country and maintained them through one or two or

24

three generations, have come to a similar
condition. The newspapers die out; the
schools, full-time and part-time, close;
the organizations, religious or secular,
shift to English; and the maintenance of
the ethnic mother tongue becomes the des-
perate struggle of a small group committed to it, who will have to find their
most effective future support less among
the descendants of the immigrants who
brought the language to this country than
in governmental and educational institutions that might find some practical or
scholarly value in training and maintaining a corps of experts who know and can
use it.

As to the erosion of ethnic tongues along the genera-
tional scale, LLUS documents what has been the normal lan-
uage experience of immigrant groups in America: the second
generation gives up the language of their parents, especially
in the many cases where the non-English tongue has been un-
pleasantly associated in the mind of the speakers with poverty, eccentricity, ignorance, and inarticulateness.

The view is advanced time and again in LLUS that language shift, or the abandonment of an ethnic tongue in favor
of English, constitutes the loss of a valuable resource. Because it has been largely through Joshua Fisman's efforts
that this view has been brought to the fore, we will equate
the sociolingustic philosophy expounded and espoused in LLUS
regarding U.S. ethnic tongues and the national interest with
that of Fishman himself. In describing Fishman's views with
respect to the national resource character of ethnic tongues
I find it useful to borrow from the terminology proposed by
W. E. Lambert to describe the type of motivation behind a
learner's desire to acquire a second language. Lambert
(1967:102-03) calls instrumental motivation that of the individual who wants to learn another tongue for utilitarian
purposes, such as getting a better position; and integrative
motivation that of the speaker whose purpose is to become
like a member of the linguistic-cultural group that speaks
that tongue. Giving the terms a slightly different connotation we could say that for Fishman, an ethnic tongue is a

national resource both instrumentally and integratively. Instrumentlly, it is to the advantage of the United States to have among its citizens people who can speak natively (and thus fluently and effectively) the languages of the foreign nations with whom this country has commercial and cultural relations, and also of course the languages of the nations with whom it has an adversary relation.

Integratively, it is to the advantage of an individual to speak the tongue of the linguistic-cultural group to which he belongs by birth, for then his existence is in Fishman's view more authentic.

Possibly no one would refute the usefulness of better communications between the United States and its allies and enemies alike. The greater authenticity of ethnic self-acceptance is equally useful but not so obvious. One could cite in support of Fishman the fact, already commonplace in social psychology, that the need to 'belong' ranks highly within the inventory of basic human needs. We will see later, however, that for some individuals ethnicity is not inseparable from language loyalty.

The Fishman volume is for the most a report on research about the status of U.S. ethnic tongues in general, with attention being given to several particular languages (viz. Spanish, German, Ukrainian, and French), but it is also in part a tract, a sort of manifesto advocating the desirability of active ethnic tongue maintenance in the United States.

Fishman's thesis could be summarized as follows: the United States, which is a multicultural nation, is also a multilingual nation, but is in danger of ceasing to be so to the detriment of all Americans. Therefore the maintenance and development of non-English tongues in the United States should be among the nation's priorities.

While aligning myself with Professor Fishman's desiderata for a multicultural-multilingual American, I would like in what follows to examine as critically as possible the question of language loyalty in the United States and explore the implications that the institutional teaching of modern languages may have for U.S. ethnic language maintenance.

Is the United States really a multilingual nation, and if so what are the dimensions of its linguistic heterogeneity? In 1970, the U.S. Bureau of the Census established that the population of this country was 203,210,258.[2] Of these, 193,590,856 were born here and 9,619,302 were foreign born. In turn, natives who gave their mother tongue as English added up to 159,019,288. While a total of 9,221,726 natives failed to report their mother tongue, 25,349,842 reported a mother tongue other than English. That is to say, in 1970 there were at least 25.3 million American-born individuals who did not speak Enlgish natively.[3] To this relatively large number add 5,125,330 foreign born U.S. residents who declared a mother tongue other than English. We arrived at the latter figure by subtracting from the total foreign born (9,619,302) the number of foreign born giving English as their mother tongue (1,697,825) and the number of foreign born who did not declare their mother tongue (96,417). And so there were at least 30 million people living in the United States in 1970 who delcared that their mother tongue was not English, roughly 15% of the population.

Table I reproduces the 1979 Census data on mother tongues of the population, ranking the languages according to the number of claimants:

TABLE I

1.	Spanish	7 823 583
2.	German	6 093 054
3.	Italian	4 144 315
4.	French	2 598 408
5.	Polish	2 437 938
6.	Yiddish	1 593 993
7.	Swedish	626 102
8.	Norwegian	612 862
9.	Slovak	510 366
10.	Greek	458 699
11.	Czech	452 812
12.	Hungarian	447 497
13.	Japanese	408 504
14.	Portugese	365 300
15.	Dutch	350 748

16.	Chinese	345 431
17.	Russian	334 615
18.	Lithuanian	292 820
19.	Ukrainian	249 351
20.	Serbo-Croatian	239 455
21.	Finnish	214 161
22.	Danish	194 462
23.	Arabic	193 520
24.	Slovenian	82 321
25.	Rumanian	56 590

The census data also include a figure of 268,205 for American Indian languages, an 'All Other' figure of 1,780,053 and a 'Not Reported' figure of 9,317,873.

The data reveal that for each of six languages other than English, there were more than one million people claiming it as their mother tongue. If we make the count progressively more inclusive, for each of nine languages there were more than half a million people; for each of 13 more than 400,000; for each of 21, more than 200,000; for each of 23, more than 150,000. These figures strike me as impressive.

We should however be as cautious as Fishmann and Hofman (1966:34) were in their analysis of 1960 mother tongue data figures:

> It should be stressed at the outset that we are dealing here primarily with self-reported mother tongue claims rather than with indicators of current language use. The two variables are undoubtedly related to each other although the exact nature or consistence of the relationship is still unknown.

Nonetheless--and Fishman and Hofman would agree--the very act of claiming a non-English tongue is quite significant.

The language problems of the United States do not seem

as pressing when compared to those of other large multilingual nations such as India, the Philippines, and the new
African nations or to those of our bilingual neighbor to the
North, Canada. The main problem afflicting many multilingual
nations--that of establishing a national language which will
function as the language of government, education, justice,
etc.--does not exist in the United States. English was
established historically as the national language long ago.
At least 79.1 per cent of the U.S. population who spoke
English natively in 1970 did not in theory have any problems
communicating with government officials, administrators of
justice, or teachers. But what about the 20 million native
speakers of non-English tongues? Many of these of course
also know English; many are bilingual to varying degrees.
Historically, however, the norm in America have been not to
make any concessions to bilinguals in the public use of
English. Historically, all systems of language communication
in America have been designed by English-speaking monolinguals who had only English-speaking monolinguals in mind.

If the medium was monolingual, the message was mono-
cultural, most significantly in education where there were
explicity directives to de-ethnicize the ethnics. For those
who may think that the inveighings against the Melting Pot
doctrine are unjustified and exaggerated, the following
passage from Krickus (1976:99) may be quite instructive:

> On graduation day it was the practice in
> some schools to conduct a ritual which
> represented the rebirth of the immigrant
> child into an American. A large pot con-
> structed out of wood and crepe paper
> stood in the center of the auditorium
> stage and the graduates entered the
> Melting Pot decked out in the apparel of
> the old country and came out the other
> side dressed resplendently in identical
> American clothes. This ritual repre-
> sented, in fact, the growing estrangement
> of the second generation from their
> parents.

The metaphor of a melting pot is actually somewhat inaccurate in describing the process that ethnics have gone

29

through in this land on their way to divesting themselves of their values, customs, and language. It would be more appropriate to speak of an Anglo-American assimilating pot. Glazer and Moynihan (1963) are right in saying that the Melting Pot did not happen. They had in mind the fact that no new American nationality has emerged from the combination of the several ethnic strains. But an assimilating process did occur and many people did come out on the other end with many more things Anglicized than their names.

On the other hand many others never went through that process. The latter were the casualties of an educational system that was not designed for them, the many non-English speaking monolinguals who never made it through the "Great School" for English-speaking monolinguals.

Nonassimilation was a common experience among so-called New Immigrants--the people from Southern and Eastern European nations who came in large numbers to America during the era of mass immigration, a period extending roughly from 1880 to 1924. (See Krickus 1976; Greer, 1972) has found that New Immigrant childen dropped out of school in large numbers with the educational failures far exceeding the successes.

These failures have been a negative source of language maintenance in America. The children who dropped out fell back into their ethnic communities where a knowledge of English was not necessary.

The experience has not been exclusive of the New Immigrants. Before the advent of publicly supported bilingual-bicultural elementary education, it was also the fate of many Puerto Rican and Mexican-American children who were largely monolingual in Spanish and of many American Indian children, equally nonproficient in the only language in which instruction was imparted.

In the history of the education of U.S. ethnics, it has turned out that diametrically opposed experiences have led in the end to the same negative results: the loss of the ethnic tongue as a resource, both instrumentally and integratively-- to refer back to Fishman's thesis in Lambertian terms. Some people who went through the Anglo-American assimilating continued to be largely monolingual in a variety of their respective languages spoken by poor and uneducated folk

30

--themselves and their elders--a variety in which it was difficult to take any pride.

Yet, it would be inaccurate to tell the history of the confrontation between Anglo-American education and ethnicity in the simple terms of an assimilated-nonassimilated dichotomy. The individual who became educated and totally rejected his ethnic heritage--including the use of his parents' tongue--and the individual who remained uneducated and monolingual in a ghettoized environment are the only extremes of an experiential range.

Of particular interest to the issue of language maintenance are the many cases of disassociation between ethnic loyalty and language loyalty. It is not true that language shift is always a manifestation of ethnic self-rejection. In the United States there are many individuals who identify themselves as members of an ethnic group, whose cultural patterns are those of that group, but who have little or no proficiency in the ethnic mother tongue. More importantly, they have little or no motivation to speak that tongue. Fishman and Nahirny (1966:186) discovered that a significant proportion of American ethnic leaders were of the opinion that "the continuity of ethnic cultural and community life in the United States may be secured without the preservation of ethnic mother tongues." (Underlining mine.) Other leaders thought otherwise but were in the minority.

Many of these leaders did not have any negative attitudes toward the fact that their own children were unwilling to speak the ethnic tongue. Many explained that the children simply did not have any opportunity to use the ethnic tongue since most of their friends and other people they spoke to knew only English.

Another symptom of the dissociation between ethnic loyalty and language loyalty is the fact that those same children of ethnic leaders did not show any negative feelings of shame or hostility toward their ethnic heritage; how different from the attitude prevailing at the same time the Anglo-American assimilating process was at its height. An ethnic writer tell us how traumatic it was:

31

> I begin to think that my grandmother is
> hopelessly a Wop. She's a small stocky
> peasant who walks with her wrists criss-
> crossed her belly, a simple old lady...
> When in her simple way, she confronts a
> friend of mine and says, her old eyes
> smiling, "You lika go to the Seester
> scola? my heart roars. Managgia! I'm
> disgraced; now they all know that I'm an
> Italian.
>
> (From John Fante's "The Oddysey of a Wop"
> (in O. Handlin (ed.) Children of the Up-
> rooted, New York: G. Braziller, 1966
> cited in Krickus (1976).

Negative attitudes toward ethnicity, on the part of
ethnics themselves and non-ethnics, have been diminishing in
the United States in the last ten years, largely through the
efforts of those engaged in the Civil Rights movement. The
Civil Right Act of 1964 put an end to the institutional dis-
enfranchisement of Black Americans, the largest U.S.
minority. Among other beneficial results for all minorities,
the official granting of equal rights to blacks was accompanied by a surge in ethnic pride. For many it meant a
healthy acceptance of their ethnic heritage, and many engaged
in a search for their ethnic roots, the cultural patterns of
their ancestors which now were seen as an inseparable part of
the individual's own identity.

Unfortunately for language maintenance, ethnic cultural
recovery did not automatically imply mother tongue recovery.
Take for instance the case of bilingual-bicultural education.
The deleterious effects of monolingual-bicultural Anglo-
American educational oppression of minorities. However, some
of the programs instituted were transitional in character.
In some cases, once the ethnic child had learned how to read
and write in his/her non-English mother tongue and had
learned English as a second language, the rest of his/her
education would be mostly in English. (See Gaarder 1970.)
Of course, this is but one model of the several that were
adopted by different publicly-funded school districts
throughout the country. The point is that bilingual-
bicultural education does not automatically imply ethnic
tongue maintenance.

32

Another manifestation of the dissociation between ethnicity and language maintenance--and one that should give pause to the language teaching profession--is the fact that the call for an educational system that takes into account the multicultural and pluralistic character of U.S. society has in general had not been accompanied by a call to study languages other than English. In a recent annotated bibliography on multicultural educational and ethnic studies in the U.S.[4], which contains abstracts of several hundred studies, less than a handful of the studies cited concern themselves with languages. It is true that the compilers of this bibliography state specifically that they are not including items on bilingual education. The point is however that the recommendation made to teachers to become aware of other cultural modes and other groups in our society (so tht they can then transmit this awareness to their students) is seldom accompanied by a recommendation to become familiar with a language other than English. It may be that many of those involved in th movement toward a multiculturally inspired public educational system in the United States are themselves ethnics who, having gone only partially through the Anglo-American assimilating process did not lose their ethnicity but did lose their ethnic tongue and would now have to study it as a foreign language.

This brings us to the relationship between foreign language teaching and language maintenance in the United States, a quite complex and problematic state of affairs.

At this time LLUS appeared, this relationship practically did not exist. In fact the neglect of U.S. ethnic tongues (and of U.S. cultural linguistic ethnic groups) extended to the field of foreign languages instruction. To my knowledge no textbook of the commonly taught languages--French, German, Italian, Russian, and Spanish--presented systematically any linguistic or cultural aspects of the varieties of these languages spoken in the United States.

At that time, foreign languages were enjoying a great deal of recognition while ethnic languages enjoyed little or none. Although it cannot be said that the situation has exactly been reversed, the fact is that today 'foreign' languages are in crisis while 'languages other than English' spoken natively in the United States are receiving attention and support--and deservingly so. Bilingual-bicultural education exists (fortunately) and in many programs instruction is conducted in the non-English ethnic tongue.

Adding to the problems of the modern language field is a dichotomy, unfavorable to the profession, which has developed among some--perhaps many--U.S. educators. It could be expressed as follows:

The Conventional Study of Foreign Languages	Attention to Ethnic Languages
Irrelevant	Relevant
Elitist	Equalitarian
Useless to society	Urgently needed by society

After years of disinterest toward non-English speaking ethnics on the part of the foreign language profession, it is no wonder that these attitudes are held, especially when the disinterest continues in many sectors of our field.

Fortunately for the foreign language field its unpopularity among ethnics is not total. It seems there are people for whom ethnics heritage recovery includes language recovery or in some cases the acquisition of a tongue connected with their heritage (e.g. Hebrew, Swahili).

A recent survey of the Modern Language Association show an increase in enrollment in many less commonly taught in U.S. colleges and universities between 1972 and 1974, the two years being compared.[5] The label 'less commonly taught' refers to languages other than Spanish, German, Italian, Russian, Latin, and Ancient Greek (which are the seven most commonly taught). This less commonly taught category includes many U.S. ethnic tongues. Enrollment figures are relatively modest. For instance Hebrew, the language with the heaviest enrollment, shows a registration total of 22,371. In some cases the figures are absolutely modest (e.g. there were nine students taking Scottish Gaelic in the U.S. in 1974).

Table II shows the language that had an enrollment greater than 1,000, ranked by their respective totals:

TABLE II

Hebrew	22,371
Chinese	10,576
Japanese	9,604
Portugese	5,073
Arabic	2,034
Swahili	1,694
Norwegian	1,557
Swedish	1,396
Polish	1,123
Yiddish	1,079

Of these, only Swahili showed a decrease (-27%) in the period 1972-1974. Of the languages listed in Table I, only Serbo-Croatian showed a decrease.

It is true that the figures of certain languages seem quite insignificant when one compares them with the number of speakers those languages have in the U.S. In addition, not every student taking a given language does so for ethnic purposes.[6]

But if at least some of the students are indeed ethnics, it is a sign which the modern language profession should welcome profusely for it means that the attitude of separating ethnic loyalty from language loyalty is not general. Or, in other words, that at least some ethnics think that the key to a group's culture is the langue spoken by the member of that culture. This, of course, has been one of the basic tenets of foreign language instruction in this of foreign language instruction in this country.

If it is true that language is the key to culture, then U.S. ethnics who 'betrayed' the ethnic mother tongue and who do not wish to recover it can never hope to completely understand themselves. If language and culture are inseparable, then U.S. ethnics who speak English natively and who are practically monolingual are more similar to other

35

English-speaking monolinguals--including Anglo-Americans--than to ethnics of their same national group who speak the ethnic tongue natively or who have acquired it as a second language.

The inextricability of language and culture would also mean that a monolingual knowing only one cultural would not be able to appreciate (and tolerate) other cultural possibilities. An educational system committed to the goals of cultural pluralism and tolerance for diversity would have to be manned by administrators and teachers who were at least bilingual. Because the people who are in a position to acquire two languages (and two cultures) exclusively from their life experiences are relatively few in number, if bilingualism for all were a societal desideratum many would have to acquire their second language in an educational setting. Clearly in such a society the teaching of non-native languages would not be regarded as irrelevant, elitist, or socially useless.

Instruction in many of the less commonly taught languages is available mainly in the self-instructional language programs that have been established throughout the country (see Boyd-Bowman 1972). As the most commonly taught languges, it is a fact that ethnics have been and continue to be attracted to conventional departments and programs where the tongue of their cultural group is taught as a foreign language.

Conventional departments are prepared--at least in theory--to attend the needs of those ethnics who are English-speaking monolinguals and who want to acquire as a second language the tongue of their cultural group which their parents or grandparents relinquished. What conventional departments are in general not prepared to do is to attend the needs of U.S. ethnics who are either monolingual in the ethnic tongue or bilingual in any degree.

What are these needs and why is a conventional department not equipped to handle them? Consider first the case of monolinguals in the ethnic tongue. In this country English-speaking monolinguals are made to take English language courses as part of their educational training. These courses are designed to improve the student's utilization of a language they already know. The results of this training show in the speech and writing of educated speakers. Had they been educated in a country where their language is the official language and is thus the medium of education, U.S. ethnic tongue monoliguals would have undergone similar training in their native tongue. But it is obvious that the methodology of teaching a foreign language differs from that of teaching native language arts. The language courses offered in a conventional foreign language department were definitely not designed for natives, and natives can profit very little from them. Many things are taught in them that a native speaker already knows. In addition, in the U.S., foreign language methodology has been contrastive, i.e., the foreign language has been taught in terms of how it approximates, or differs from, English. For ethnics who do not know English, being subjected to contrastive instruction is absurd. (For a clear discussion of the methodological differences between native and foreign language instruction, see Fallis 1976.)

What about bilingual ethnics? Logically, conventional instruction is equally irrelevant for them if they are ethnic tongue dominant. But it is beneficial to them if they are English-dominant? Ethnics who know English and in addition have at least a passive knowledge of their ethnic tongue would in theory be better off than an English monolingual who starts at zero. In practice, however, the ethnic finds he does not have any advantage, for even though the tongue which he partially knows and that taught in the book go by the same name, they turn out to be different versions and the book is deemed to be the correct one.

Unfavorable comparisons between an ethnic's lect and the standard are not limited to the lower levels of conventional instruction (i.e. the langue course per se) but are also encountered at the more advanced levels, especially in literature courses. Academic recruitment of minorities have brought many of the U.S. ethnic poor to college degree programs. Those who are ethnic tongue-dominant take courses in literature in conventional foreign language departments. (This is especially true of Puerto Ricans and Chicanos vis-à-vis departments where Spanish is taught.) But conventional literature courses are designed for students who have both a college level reading ability and (at least in theory) a mastery of the standard form of the language in which its literature is written. Since the ethnic poor normally have

37

neither, their performance in these courses is below average and they are penalized with low or failing grades. This is perceived by many ethnics as a manifestation of discrimination, a perception that is probably reinforced by the fact that conventional departments do not normally provide any type of remedial instruction that would prevent or alleviate those failures.

An issue greatly relevant to the related questions of language loyalty and language maintenance is the one surrounding the exclusive use in conventional foreign language instruction of the standard variety of the language. Traditionally, many educators have had what Shuy (1969) has called an attitude of eradication vis-á-vis nonstandard lects. (See also Fallis 1976.) For the eradictors, the role of language is to replace nonstandard forms by standard ones. In recent years sociolinguists have been proposing that educators embrace instead the goal of 'functional bidialectalism' or biloquialism, as Shuy (1969) calls it, and which he describes as "a person's right to continue speaking the dialect of his home (which may be nonstandard) even after he has learned a school dialect (which may be standard)."

Shuy was speaking primarily of standard and nonstandard forms of English but, as Fallis (1976) has shown, the terms are entirely applicable to the situation of non-English tongue ethnics in the U.S. Very probable because of their negative experiences with eradicators, non-English tongue ethnics have come to equate any proposals in favor of standard usage with the constellation of prejudices regarding nonstandard forms. This has coupled with an emerging ethnic pride to create among certain ethnics the attitude that biloquialism is an irrelevant goal. This attitude is examplified in the response given by the Chicano linguist, Eduardo Hernandez-Chavez to a report issued by the American Association of Teachers of Spanish and Portugese, advocating the teaching of Spanish to its native speakers in the U.S. The writer of that report, A. Bruce Gaarder, saw as a major linguistic goal "to give the learner full command and literacy in world standard Spanish" (cited in Lovas 1975:119.) Wrote Hernandez Chavez:

> ... our primary rationale for learning and maintaining Spanish is not so that it will serve as a link to Latin America, but so

that it will become a strengthening and
reinforcing bond for chicanismo within our
own communities. Standard Spanish will
not only detract us from this goal, it
will be an alienating factor. We cannot
go into our communities to talk to the
people in standard Spanish and expect to
effectively gain a feeling of confianza
and carnalismo. To do this naturally and
effectively, we must use the language of
the people, our language, Pocho.

Lovas, 1975: 119

When Weinreich developed the concept of language loyalty
he had in mind the attitudes of purists rallying around a
standard. If Hernandez-Chavez' response is a reflection of
widespread feelings among Chicanos, it would mean then that
they are loyal to a nonstandard. But does 'dialect loyalty'
lead to language maintenance the way language loyalty does?

The answer would seem to be no. A standard is easy to
defend and promote because of its 'visibility'. Being high
codified, it is susceptible of improvement and refinement,
including the conscious elimination of interference from
other languages. But in a situation of language contact in
the U.S. nothing stands between a noncodified lect and further Anglification.

It is almost axiomatic that language as a tool for wider
communication can be improved. In discussing the properties
that a standard should have in order to function efficiently,
Garvin (1960:784) includes that of 'intellectualization'
which he describes as a "tendency towards increasingly more
definite and accurate expression". He goes on to say:

In the lexicon, intellectualization manifests itself by increased terminological
precision achieved by the development of
more clearly differentiated terms. In
grammar, intellectualization manifests itself by the development of word formation
techniques and of syntactic devices allow-
ing for the construction of elaborate, yet
tightly knit, compound sentences, as well

39

> as the tendency to eliminate elliptic
> modes of expression by requiring complete
> constructions. (Garvin 1950:785).

Intellectualization would of course not be possible without codification, but codification and intellectualization are mutually supportive. The written language is the best vehicle for the improvement of expression, and improvement of expression in turn improves the code itself.

Yet in the highly charged atmosphere surrounding the standard vs. nonstandard issue, it is tantamount to an insult to say that communication in a nonstandard variety stands little chance of improvement and refinement if no effort is made for it to approach the standard code.

Surely, Fishman (1966:379) was in no way trying to insult Italian Americans when among his specific recommendations for language maintenance in the United States he included the following:

> "Old Country" contact with naturalized
> citizens and their children should be fos-
> tered under favorable national circum-
> stances. Italian governmental efforts to
> keep Italian language, literature, and
> customs alive may be thought of as a form
> of reverse lend-lease and may very well be
> a form of debt-repayment. Such efforts
> help to keep Italian alive <u>and closer to
> its standardization form among Italo-
> Americans. They help overcome the con-
> stant Anglification and petrification that
> obtains when a language of immigrants does
> not have all of the normal avenues for
> use, growth, and change.</u> (Underlining
> mine.)

It was only natural that in his recommendation Fishman did not include approaching conventional Italian departments in this country where the standard form of the language was taught and its literary monuments studies, for reasons we discussed in the foregoing. If he were to formulate his recommendations today he would still leave conventional departments out of the picture since in general there has been little change in the relationship (or lack of relation-ship) between the field of modern languages and U.S. ethnics. I am referring of course to languages in general, not only Italian.

If the United States were to adopt a language planning policy that had as its specific goal the maintenance and de-velopment of U.S. ethnic tongues, it could not turn for ex-pertise to the modern language field. The methodology for teaching ethnic language arts in the U.S. is still in its in-fancy and there is no general movement on the part of con-ventional departments to aid in its development. Furthermore eradicationist attitudes have in general not abated. No in-stitutional reapproachment between U.S. ethnics and the foreign language field is in sight. Add to the list of symp-toms of this fact that bilingual-bicultural educational efforts have had institutionally very little to do with lan-guage departments. In what little language planning there exists in the United States today (i.e., bilingual-bicultural education), the foreign language field has been largely left out. And yet if some significant attitudinal and methodo-logical changes were to be made,[7] what more adequate place to train teachers in the language and culture of a group than a language department, and what more adequate place to turn student into educated users of their own native language?

It seems, however, that those changes are not going to be made--at least not in the immediate future--and that lan-guage departments will continue to leave themselves out of the picture as far as organized U.S. ethnic language main-tenance efforts are concerned.

NOTES

1. I would like to thank very especially Paul Garvin, Wolf-gang and Andreas Gallardo for their helpful suggestions. I am entirely responsible for any omissions and errors.

2. The source for this and all other Census figures was 1970 Census of the Population, Characteristics of the Population, United States Summay, United States Department of Commerce, 1973.

3. Recent U.S. Bureau of the Census estimates, which became available to me after this paper was practically completed, give a more revealing picture of the extent of multilingualism (and of individual bilingualism) in the United States. They are also revealing of the extent of 'language betrayal'. In a Survey of Languages conducted as a supplement of the monthly Current Population Survey in July, 1975, the estimated number of persons aged four and older living in households where languages other than English are spoken is 28,655,000. Of these, 25,344,000 are native Americans. Of the latter group, 1,328,000 live in households where English is not spoken at all, and 24,064,000 in households where both English and a non-English language are spoken. At the same time only 6,9414,000 of the latter live in households where a non-English tongue is the usual language and 17,573,000 live in households where English is the usual language. For a detailed interpretation of these estimates see Waggoner (1976) from whom I have taken all figures.

4. Multicultural Education and Ethnic Studies in the United States: A Anaylsis and Annotated Bibliography of Selected Documents in ERIC, Ethnic Heritage Center for Teacher Education, American Association of Colleges Education, 1976.

5. The source for the results of the survey was "Enrollments in less commonly taught languages, U.S. Colleges and Universities, Fall of 1974" in A.D.F.L, Bulletin of the Association of Departments of Foreign Languages, Vol. 7, No. 3, March 1976.

6. In the Critical Languages Program that Professor Peter Boyd-Bowman, directs at my institution, the students' ethnicity determines in general their choice in the case of Hebrew and certain European languages (e.g. Polish) but not in general in the case of Oriental languages (e.g. Japanese). (Peter Boyd-Bowman, personal communication).

7. For a very interesting proposal concerning the creation of a new interdisciplinary field that would encompass both conventional language study and attention to the language needs of U.S. ethnic minorities, see Lambert (1975).

REFERENCES

Boyd-Bowman, Peter. 1972. National self-instructional program in Critical Languages. Modern Languages Journal
56:164:7.

Fallis, Guadalupe V. 1976. Pedagogical implications of
teaching Spanish to the Spanish-speaking in the United
States. In: Teaching Spanish to the Spanish speaking:
Theory and practice, ed by Guadalupe Valdes Fallis and
Rudolfo Garcia Moya, Trinity University, San Antonio.
3-27.

Fishman, Joshua A. 1966. Planned reinforcement of language
maintenance in the United States: suggestions for the
conservation of a neglected national resource, In:
Fishman et al, 369-91.

_____ and Vladimir C. Nahirny, John E. Hofman, and Robert
G. Hayden. 1966. Language loyalty in the U.S. The
Hague: Mouton.

_____ and John E. Hofman. 1966. Mother tongue and nativ-
ity in the American population. In: Fishman et al, 34-
50.

_____ and Vladimir C. Nahirny. 1966. Organizational and
leadership interest in language maintenance. In: Fishman et at, 156-89.

Gaarder, A. Bruce. 1970. The first seventy-six bilingual
projects. In: Georgetown University Round Table on Languages and Linguistics 1970, ed. by James Alatis.
Georgetown University Press. 163-78.

Garvin, Paul L. 1960. The urbanization of the Guarani--a
problem in language and culture. In: Anthony F. C.
Wallace, ed. Men and Cultures, Selected papers of the
Fifth International Congress of Anthropological and Eth-
nological Sciences. Philadelphia: University of Pennsylvania Press. 783-90.

Glazer, Nathan. 1966. The process and problems of language

maintenance: an integrative review. In: Fishman et al, 358-68.

_____ and Daniel P. Moynihan. 1963. Beyond the melting pot. Cambridge: M.I.T. Press.

Greer, Colin. 1972. The great school legend. New York: Basic Books.

Krickus, Richard. 1976. Pursuing the American Dream: white ethnics and the new populism. Garden City: Anchor Books, Anchor-Doubleday.

Lambert, Wallace E. 1967. A social psychology of bilingualism. The Journal of Social Issues 23:91-109.

_____. 1975. An alternative to the foreign language teaching profession. Lektos 1, No. 2: 1-15.

Lovas, John C. 1975. Language planning in a multilingual community in the U.S. In: New directions in second language learning, teaching and bilingual education, ed. by Marina K. Burt and Heidi C. Dulay. TESOL, Washington, D.C. 113-22.

Shuy, Roger W. 1969. Bonnie and Clyde tactics in English teaching. The Florida FL Reporter 7:81-3, 160-1.

Waggoner, Dorothy. Results of the Survey of Languages Supplement to the July 1975 Current Population Survey. A paper presented at the Fifth Annual International Bilingual Bicultural Education Conference, San Antonio, Texas, May 4, 1976.

CHAPTER 3

LANGUAGE DEVELOPMENT VERSUS THE TEACHING OF THE

STANDARD LANGUAGE

Guadalupe Valdés
New Mexico State University

Some time ago, at the beginning of the 1975-76 academic year to be exact, a medium-sized southwestern university was faced with the following problem: it had received ten fellowships which were to support ten Mexican-Americans students through doctoral studies in bilingal education. It was assumed that these students would be "Spanish-speaking"; but since interview and selection procedures were typical of these programs in general, it turned out that while these young persons could communicate superficially in Spanish, the majority of them were completely incapable of teaching classes in this language in the variety of subjects which make up the ordinary elementary school curriculum. Several of the fellows felt that they could read in Spanish with some degree of comfort, but most confessed that they could not read at all, could not spell correctly, and very few even dared to attempt a conversation in Spanish on topics of general academic interest.

Very briefly, each one of these doctoral students, veteran teachers of bilingual education programs, were simply English dominant. The question was: What could be done with these students? What methods, courses, etc., were available that would result in the needed fluency for these teachers (all of whom, to the person, were committed to language maintenance programs in bilingual education)? The southwestern university had no answers. The college of education was not equipped to take on such a task and its efforts were limited to teaching a number of "bilingual methods" courses in both English and Spanish. On the other hand, the department of Spanish had not ever before been faced with such a practical problem. Like universities all over the United States, this department was designed around the teaching of Spanish to non-speakers, that is, as a foreign language and around the production of the traditional Spanish major. Courses therefore included: beginning and intermediate Spanish for non-speakers, advanced conversation, advanced grammar and composition, and principally some ten or more courses in Latin American and peninsular literature. The only concession made to the fact that this university was surrounded by native speakers of the Spanish language was a two-semester course (Spanish 213-214) entitled Spanish for Spanish-speaking students, with which Mexican-American students could not fulfill their language requiement and not compete with the beginning non-speaking students.

It was evident when faced with the problem of placing the ten doctoral students mentioned above, that there was not even a single course which could provide these students with the overall development in the language which they so desperately needed. The course designed for under-graduate native-speaking students was not at all well-defined. It generally depended on the specific instructor in the course, whether the emphasis would be placed on teaching grammatical terminology, teaching a standard dialect, or the teaching of basic reading and writing skills. At the same time the course in advanced conversation used a text designed to elicit ordinary speech for traveling, ordering meals, etc., at a level already mastered by all of these doctoral students. The advanced grammar and composition course, on the other hand, was aimed at future teachers of the Spanish language as a foreign language. Thus the emphasis was placed on a review of traditional grammar and on perfecting elementary skills in the area of written Spanish. Indeed it was soon apparent that while many of the courses in literature or even in linguistics would help, they simply were not designed for the task at hand. Everyone agreed that the undergraduate course for native-speakers could be recommended only for those doctoral students whould could not read and write at all, but to this day (with a new crop of fellows in the wings) the question is still being pondered.

The purpose of this paper then is to center the attention of the foreign language teaching profession on this problem: the problem of the language development and language growth of the English dominant, Spanish-speaking student who hopes to increase his total command of the Spanish language for the purpose of functioning in that language at a level equivalent to that of most educated Latin Americans. I will therefore examine the two principle existing approaches in teaching ethnic students in their mother tongue. I will examine the time-honored emphasis on the teaching of traditional grammar, the new-found interest in teaching ethnic students the "standard" dialect of their mother tongue, and finally I will compare each of these approaches and its results with that of a program in language development which would have as its principal objective the overall growth in proficienty by the student.

The Teaching of Traditional Grammar

Despite recent advances in the theory of language acquisition and generative grammar, etc., for most language teachers the question: "What does it mean to know a language?" is best answered by the time-honored view that to <u>know</u> a language is to <u>know consciously</u> and <u>express verbally</u> exactly how it functions within a system of traditional grammar. Thus, it is not unusual to find that of a teacher of the Spanish language will often complain that a fluent native-speaking student of the language in a particular class knows less Spanish than an English-speaking monolingual (with perhaps two semesters' study in the language) simply because the native speaker cannot verbalize exactly how he is using his language. It is not sufficient for the instructor to observe that the native-speaker will never <u>ser</u> and <u>estar</u>, always observes the rules of verb/subject agreement noun/-adjective agreement, etc. If the native speaker cannot list the rules verbatim, he is told that he does not <u>know</u> his language. In many cases instructors go so far <u>as to</u> say that third-semester English monolinguals studying Spanish will "write" more competently than Spanish-speaking students in the same class. When questioned further it turns out that the elaborateness of well-formed sentences produced by the Spanish-speaking students cannot be matched by the former group, it is only that "writing" to some instructors mean <u>spelling</u> and not <u>composition</u>. Thus, when faced with designing a course for these Spanish-speaking students, it is not unusual for a department or for a lone instructor, given that responsibility, to decide what this student needs is a text in traditional grammar which from the very beginning will teach him what every item in his language is known as to the traditional grammarian. Instruction then is devoted to endless definitions of articles, adjectives, nouns, verbs, etc., and testing involves rote recognition of parts of speech, listings of verb paradigms (which are often clearly a part of these speakers' everyday language) and verbalizations of rules and more rules and exceptions to the exceptions. Whatever writing is done is limited. The student is given a little credit for the skills he brings with him, and at the end, success is achieved if these students manage to resemble as far as possible the products of the traditional intermediate courses for non-speakers. Indeed they are well on their way to becoming more and more like all other traditional Spanish "majors," the principal product of such departments.

Unfortunately, it does not occur to these instructors or to these departments that while such a grounding in traditional grammar is essential, at this time, for those persons going on to major in the language and perhaps going on to teach traditional grammar themselves, it is of little value for those students who are simply taking a course in order to develop their existing limited skills. If these students can be offered a means by which they can develop their total language skills (speaking, understanding, reading and writing), and in addition to that learn to recognize the niceties of its structure well and good. But if one must choose between learning how to recognize what one does when one uses ser vs estar or the preterite vs the imperfect and being able to read comfortably in the language (due to extended and varied practice), then the choice is clear, minority Spanish--speaking students who do not want to be Spanish majors, but who want to maintain and build on their existing skills are not being aided in the process by simply being made to talk about areas in which they never or seldom err. They will and do learn what is taught them-but seen against an entire lifetime, as perhaps the only opportunity to "study" Spanish formally, it can be a tragic waste. Progress will only be made if departments of language will stop looking at each course as having to prepare the student for the courses which follow. In other words, simply because there may be a course in advanced grammar at the junior level, this does not mean that every course at the sophomore level need be taught as if the student were going on to this specific advanced course. Perspective majors can very easily be told which courses must be taken prior to enrolling in the required grammar sequence. Other courses can and must exist which offer student other alternatives.

The Teaching of the Standard Dialect as a Second Dialect

I have mentioned elsewhere (Valdés-Fallis, 1975, 1976) that for some time the foreign language teaching profession has not concerned itself with teaching ethnic students their mother tongue. But even today the newly awakened interest which arose in the wake of the civil rights movement and the current emphasis on cultural pluralism is still largely concerned with correcting the damage that has been done at home. Indeed if the language teacher is concerned at all with the oral proficiency of these students it is only to point out that this oral language is different and therefore inferior to the "standard" dialect of the language. Sadly enough, the precedents already well-established within the English-profession by Kochman (1974), Sledd (1969, 1972), Shuy (1971, 1973), Steward (1970), Goodman (1976), and Underwood (1974) concerning second-dialect teaching and dialect erradication have had little or no impact on these departments. Indeed it would seem that the profession, and especially departments of Spanish are laboring under the following delusions (which have already been widely discussed within the English teaching profession):

1. That bidialectalism is a desirable end in itself, in that, in order to be truly quality Spanish-speaking persons, U.S. Hispanos must speak like Spaniards or Latin Americans who have both power and social prestige in their own countries. (In other words they must sound like upper-class Madrilenos or Bonairenses).

2. That it is possible to "teach" a second dialect in a classroom setting, And,

3. That dialect differences are numerous and serious.

I will not repeat here the arguments which I have put forth elsewhere (Valdés-Falls, 1976) concerning the problems underlying each of the above assumptions. Suffice it to say, that there is no evidence whatsoever that a given dialect is inferior or superior to any other. Prestige comes not from the dialect itself but from the social position of its speakers. In the case of Mexican-American students for example, it is a well-known fact that they are not going to enjoy a wide acceptance in Mexico by the upper classes, regardless of what dialect of Spanish they speak. On the other hand, a large number of Mexican citizens and Latin American citizens speak a dialect which (with a few exceptions) is identical to that spoken by U.S. Hispanos. If bidialectalism is desirable, it is not desirable because the native-dialect is unsuitable or inferior. It is desirable because, for the Spanish-speaking student, it can theoretically offer a wide range of experiences in his lifetime.

The arguments put forth by the CCC in its very vital issue entitled "Student's Right to Their Own Language," (1974) are as valid for Spanish and every other minority language as they are for English. Unfortunately, it will take some time before members of any of these professions come to realize that edited written language necessarily differs from the spoken language. Indeed instruction must involve teaching the student where written and spoken language differ, but it would seem important for instructors to be aware of the fact that both the prestige variant of a given language and its non-prestige variants differ from the standard edited form.

My own personal objections to making the teaching of the standard dialect as a second dialect the principal thrust of the Spanish-teaching profession in the teaching of U.S. Hispanos has to do with the three principal factors:

1. We do not know for a fact that a second dialect can be taught. We know that it can be learned, but up to this point, it has not been demonstrated that it can successfully be taught in a classroom setting. Indeed, both Shuy (1971, 1973) and Steward (1969, 1970) have made clear the fact that quasi-foreign language methods can be confusing and ineffectual simply because bidialectalism implies dialect appropriateness and it is difficult to create (in a classroom setting) the various contexts within which each dialect would be considered naturally appropriate.

2. While there has been much talk concerning the importance of self-image to the extent that elementary schools throughout the country are being aware that to demand English of a non-English-speaking child

51

when he enters school may make him feel that there is something seriously wrong with either himself, his parents, his background, or his language, there has been less talk concerning what happens to, for example, a Chicano student who is very clearly made to feel that his dialect of Spanish is simply not the "right" one. If we are concerned with language maintenance among ethnic minorities (and perhaps that is open to question), then we must be concerned with the fact that minority students do not become convinced that the mother tongue they bring with them is not worth maintaining.

3. Second dialect teaching as a principal thrust within a language teaching program does little to encourage and promote overall growth in the language as a whole. This is not to say that dialect differences would not be mentioned. This simply means that in the same way that a student who learns grammatical terminology exclusively during a semester, the student who learns standard dialect equivalents for each of his "non-standard" forms exclusively has added little to his ability in speaking, understanding, reading, and writing. With very few exceptions, he is exactly where he was before in terms of functional potential.

In the final chapter of this paper, I will attempt to further clarify the above point.

Three Instructional Options and the Lingusitic Characteristics of the English-Dominant, Spanish-Speaking Bilingual

In this section, I will discuss the two instructional options already mentioned as well as a third option: the total language development program. While I will be using examples from the U.S. Hispano experience, the parallels will be obvious for the teaching of most other "minority" languages in the United States.

Figure I (adapted from Clyne, 1967) represents the relative Spanish and English language proficiency of the English-dominant, Spanish-speaking student. Because of his English-

52

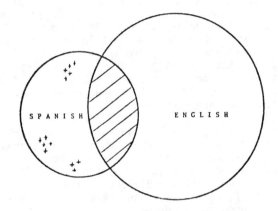

 Overlap Spanish/English (Vocabulary
belonging to both systems)

 Non-standard features

FIGURE I

THE ENGLISH-DOMINANT U.S. BILINGUAL

53

language, public school education, the secondary school-age bilingual is, with very few exceptions, English dominant. His spanish vocabulary is restricted to the home, neighborhood, and perhaps church domain; while his English vocabularly encompasses his intellectual and abstract thought, his interaction with the majority culture (the working world, the media, etc.). Because he is bilingual, this type of student has a large area of overlap; that is, of vocabulary which the bilingual may have trouble identifying as belonging to only one of his languages. Thus he may use a series of loan words, loan translations, etc., fully convinced that they are truly Spanish items. As a member of bilingual speech community his Spanish contains a large number of integrated borrowings which are in fact part of the Spanish variant that his community speaks. This contrasts with spontaneous transfer or interference (which is not the norm in his community) but which is characteristic of all persons whose languages are in contact.

In addition, the Spanish dialect or variant of this speaker is characterized by a number of features which are not found in the standard dialect of the Spanish language, that is, in edited written Spanish. It is important to notice, however, that the dialect or variant of this student shares many features with the same standard Spanish. Contrary to popular opinion, there is no one-to-one correspondence between Chicano or Puerto Rican Spanish and written edited Spanish. There are no "non-standard" translations for all standard Spanish sentences, and it is quite impossible to give non-standard equivalences for mathematical, geographical, or sociological terminology. Indeed, depending upon the register in use by a particular Chicano or Puerto Rican speaker, the most formal to the most informal within his own specific variety, most of his utterances may be quite identical with the written edited language.

Figure II represents the first instructional option discussed above, the teaching of traditional grammar. As can be seen in the diagram, the overall proficiency in English and Spanish remains the same. In essence, what the student learns to do is speak about the Spanish that he already speaks. In many cases he may learn rules for using tenses or moods which may not be characteristic of his spoken dialect at all. Possibly such instruction may make clear to him the

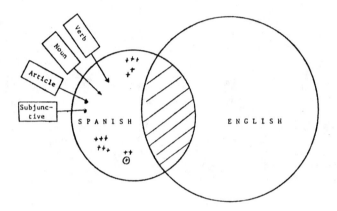

Overlap Spanish/English (Vocabulary belonging to both systems)

Non-standard features [some may be recognized as such]

Traditional grammar tags [the student can now speak about the language]

FIGURE II

INSTRUCTIONAL OPTION A: THE TEACHING OF TRADITIONAL GRAMMAR

fact that certain items (say the radical-changing verbs) are regularized in his dialect and not in the standard. Very clearly then, if one seeks to provide instruction which will provide growth in all areas of the Spanish language experience, such instruction is not an ideal choice.

Instruction which has as its central purpose the erradication or correction of non-standard features as well as the erradication of the items brought about by the overlap of the two languages would resemble that depicted by Figure III. Very obviously the general use of competence in the Spanish language remains the same. Instruction is designed so that the student can identify each and every one of his non-standard features and hopefully remember them long enough to pass an examination at the end of the semester. If the student is fortunate, he will also receive instruction in spelling and reading in addition to tedious explanations based upon traditional grammar. In the best of cases, the above student will be able to take his place among Spanish majors, and teach the language as a foreign language or even as a second dialect, having been well versed in all the current "errors." But seldom will he feel that he has in fact gained much in his overall knowledge and fluency.

It is evident, however, that second dialect instruction cannot really help the student guard himself against every incident of spontaneous interference. Using word lists, drills, etc., such instruction may make some headway against the commonly recognized integrated forms used by such bilingual speakers, but it cannot create two perfect monolingual speakers out of a bilingual speaker. His two languages are and will be in contact, and until such time as his weaker language grows and is strengthened to the degree that he is not "at a loss for words" in this language, he will continue to spontaneously create terms when he needs them. Indeed, this may and does happen to even so-called "balanced" bilinguals.

In essence then, instruction dedicated to the goals depicted in Figure III seem dubious at best, and for the Spanish-teaching profession to put its eggs into this one basket in the light of what we have learned in the past decade about second dialect teaching is criminally incompetent. For all the beautiful materials we can produce for all the asinas we may change to and the puedmos to

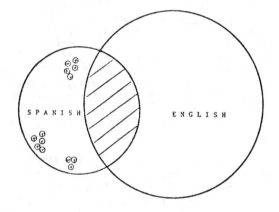

 Overlap (Student memorizes long lists of stigmatized "anglicisms"); RESULT: Student guards against integrated forms but cannot guard himself against spontaneous interference

Each type of non-standard feature is analyzed and corrected

FIGURE III

INSTRUCTIONAL OPTION B: TEACHING STANDARD FEATURES FOR ALL NON-STANDARD FEATURES (TEACHING THE STANDARD DIALECT AS A SECOND DIALECT)

57

podemos, etc., we will not have solved the problem of the bilingual speaker who wants to increase his total command of his first language.

Figure IV represents a third instructional option. Within such instruction the primary objective is the development of the Spanish language to resemble the development of the English language as a whole. Attention is devoted to increasing oral command of the language, to writing (orthography), to composition, to creative use of the language, to reading skills, and to exposure to numerous topics and domains which are normally handled by the student in his dominant language. If non-standard features are mentioned at all, they are mentioned as variants which, while existing in the spoken language, are never written except when consciously imitating such specific speech patterns. Examples of such items are tavia, pa, sia bia visto, etc. The aim of the instruction as a whole is to develop total command of the first language, including a mastery of edited, written Spanish.

Very obviously, such an aim is a difficult one, and very certainly as inaccessible in the majority of departments of Spanish in the U.S. as it was in the specific southwestern university of which I spoke above. Such instruction would take time, effort, planning, and above all, an individualization of requirements and activities to suit the specific capabilities of each student. For some students, who are simply receptive bilinguals, the process would be long and hard. But for others, a carefully designed program could build upon existing skills and move foreward. The questions are: How long would it take? How much would it cost? Who would be qualified for such a program? and What would have to be eliminated in order to bring such instruction about?

I confess that I do not have clear-cut answers to all of these questions I am convinced, however, that they must be answered. If the profession can be convinced that instruction does not have to begin with remodeling the inner Spanish core of the bilingual student before proceeding to develop the language in general, they will be answered. In past decades, a number of applied linguists have found ways to increase the effectiveness of language training programs for non-speakers. If they have been able to produce

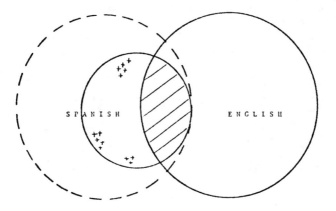

Spanish area expanded to approximate English area
— — — (Growth takes place in speaking, understanding,
reading and writing)

 "Anglicisms" are not "corrected." While the overlap
area expands, Spanish vocabularly exceeds the vocabulary of the overlap area significantly; Spontaneous
interference will continue to occur

Non-standard features are not "corrected"; Standard
features far exceed non-standard features; All growth
has taken place in the standard language

FIGURE IV

INSTRUCTIONAL OPTION C: DEVELOPING PROFICIENCY TO
APPROXIMATE ENGLISH EFFICIENCY

competent communicating personnel for various functions, certainly it is not beyond us to produce qualified bilingual teachers who can in fact bring about minority language maintenance in this country. We need only stop to think that there are other reasons for teaching language than those in which we have involved ourselves in the past. We must examine the student before us and his needs and then design our programs and our materials. We cannot continue to insist the students become assembly-ling products of an outdated and perhaps irrelevant machine.

REFERENCES

Clyde, Michael G. 1967. Transference and triggering. The Martinus Nijhoff.

Goodman, Kenneth S. Reading: A psycholinguistic guessing game. Current topics of language, ed. by N. A. Johnson. 370-383. Cambridge, Mass.: Winthrop Publishers.

Kochman, Thomas. 1974. Standard English revisted or who's kidding/cheating who(m). F.F.L.R. 12. 31-44, 96.

Shuy, Roger. 1971. Social dialects: Teaching vs. learning. F.F.L.R. 9. 28-33, 55.

Shuy, Roger. 1973. Some useful myths in social dialectology. F.F.L.R. 11. 17-20, 55.

Sledd, James. 1969. Bi-dialectalism: The linguisitics of white supremacy. English journal. 58. 1307-1315.

Sledd, James. 1971. Doublespeak: Dialectology in the service of big brother. College English. 33. 439-57.

Stewart, William A. 1969. Lanugage teaching problems in Appalachia. F.F.L.R. 7. 58-59, 161.

Stewart, William A. 1970. Foreign language teaching methods in quasi-foreign language situations. Teaching standard English in the inner city, ed. by R. W. Fasold and R. Shuy, 1-19. Washington, D.C.: Center for Applied Linguistics.

Students' right to their own language. 1974. Journal of the conference on college composition and communication. 25. 1-32.

Underwood, Gary R. 1974. Bidialectal freshman handbooks—the next film flam. F.F.L.R. 12. 45-58, 97, 99.

_____. 1975. Teaching Spanish to the Spanish-speaking: Classroom strategies. System. 3. 54-62.

_____. 1976. Pedagogical implications of teaching Spanish to the Spanish-speaking. Teaching Spanish to the Spanish-speaking: Theory and practice, ed. by Guadalupe Valdes-Fallis, 5-27. San Antonio, Texas: Trinity University.

CHAPTER 4

LANGUAGE AND POLITICAL SOCIALIZATION IN A BICULTURAL SOCIETY

Robert St. Clair and James Eiseman
University of Louisville

INTRODUCTION

Every society faces the common problem of introducing its citizens to the power elite and its control of the political system, its dominance over the military establishment, and its maintenance over the corporate structure (Prewitt and Stone, 1973). This insures that each new generation of infants will partake in the common image of a benevolent government and not resist the status quo. This process is so successful that by the time a child is in the eighth grade, he or she is thoroughly politicized (Easton and Dennis, 1969). They begin by viewing their own parents as figures of authority and gradually come to accept other forms of authority in the personalized figures of the President of the United States and the policeman. This apprentice citizen will progress from stage to stage of political maturation and finally reach chronological adulthood where full legal status is bestowed by the host society.

For the immigrant who arrives into a new nation as an adult, the process of Americanization takes on a different form of politicization. This individual already has a different set of political attitudes and social expectations. This state of dual allegiance creates special problems for those who view them as potential members of the work force. They lack in the rudiments of literacy in the new languge; their loyalty is to their ethnic group; and, their values are imbued in the native languages. In addition, their patterns of social interaction sometimes conflict and this leads to a state of bicultural dissonance (Novotny, 1974). It is for this reason that what some interpret as a purely linguistic task of teaching English to the immigrants is a well-defined socio-political activity (Thompson, 1971). In a capitalistic nation where value is equated with financial gain, this process of Americanization is directly tied to the needs of labor and the commercial gains of the ruling elite (Jones, 1974: Bowles and Gintis, 1976).

As one begins to study the language of the school system and how it portrays life in socio-economic terms, it becomes readily apparent that the medium of expression is integrated into a hidden curriculum which imparts the ideals of a silent culture. It is for this reason that the study of language in a bicultural society is informative and can provide insight into social history, political socialization, the legitimation of knowledge, and social control.

LANGUAGE EDUCATION IN THE COLONIAL SETTING

When the East India Company established its colonial administration in the subcontinent of Eurasia, it attempted a unique experiment. It began a program for teaching English as a foreign language. What makes this experiment so unique is that its scope was directed at a whole nation (Basu, 1978). The immediate concern, however, was to work with the elite among the populace of India and train them in the language of the colonial master, the literature of the metropole, and the culture and history of England. This policy of British imperialism was most effective in the schools where the curriculum that they imposed on their Indian subjects enabled them to maintain better control of the labor force and the commerce of trade. Implicit in this new form of education, however, was the underlying adherence to a form of social Darwinism which boasted of a superior literature, the myth of Teutonic supremacy, an enriched system of jurisprudence, and demonstrations of military force.

The focus of the managerial elite was two-fold. In order to establish control, these local subjects must continue to maintain social distance with the masses. Not only was this accomplished, but the new managerial elite were so intent on emulating the British in both language and culture that their new social class took on a tinge of mystery and prestige. They spoke with a British accent, they dressed in the manner of their new masters, and they immersed themselves in the literature of England. However, their quest for social status among the colonial administrators was never to be realized.

64

The colonial administrators of India did not want to mingle with the managerial elite of the country. They also wanted to maintain social distance. They created barriers to social mobility and carefully controlled the status of the members to their newly formed social clubs. The result of this politics of control is that the local managerial elites found themselves in a state of double alienation. They were no longer a part of their own people with its traditions and communal values and they could never become a part of the lives of the administrators of the East India Company. The significance of this form of social control through language and education in India is that it represents the classical case of colonialism.

The model of classical colonalism was not limited to the British experience. Other countries soon learned to use this process of political socialization and accomplished this rather effectively. The French, for example, have utilized these tactics of control and legitimation in Algeria (Fanon, 1952; 1961; Memmi, 1968). In this case the love of the metropole became a driving force among the colonized managerial elite who went to Paris to study, read the literature of France, and partook of its civilization. In Vietnam, there was a similar approach to class domination, however, some of the differences encountered in Southeast Asia merit further discussion. In discussing the colonization of Vietnam, Gail Kelly (1978) notes how in the beginning both Vietnamese and French children went to the same school to learn the literature and the customs of the metropole and to acquire a proficiency in the French language. An interesting state of affairs developed, however, which the French colonials apparently overlooked. The Vietnamese children turned out to be excellent students and surpassed the children of the French administrators. When the time came for these students to compete for high education in the metropole, it was the Vietnamese that dominated in the battery of tests. Hence, in order to insure their supremacy and regain their dominance, the French imposed a bilingual literacy act that required children to be trained in their native languages at the elementary level. This mean that the Vietnamese would go to schools in which French was not used as the medium of instruction and where the informative details of culture and history were lacking. The expectation of such legislation should be readily apparent. When both groups came together at the middle school level, it was the

65

children of the colonial administrators who met with extraordinary success. This is a basic strategy in the politics of literacy.

INTERNAL COLONIALISM

Another form of colonialism occurs when the people who are oppressed reside within the metropole. An obvious case of this form of political socialization can be found in the Indian reservation system within the United States. It has all of the characteristics of classical colonialism. It is administered by a colonial force that does not belong to the tribal community and does not share in its values and sense of history. It has imposed its foreign language and its alien culture on its subjects and controls their access to the mainstream of their socio-economic system by means of literacy requirements which are mediated in a foreign language. This form of hegemony serves to keep the native populace of the reservation system at the bottom of the social structure while creating the positive image of benevolent paternalism.

Katherine Iverson (1978) has aptly described the process of internal colonialism and notes how the formal education of Native Americans has always had as its intent the radical change of these societies for the purpose of promoting order in the larger economic and political system. In addition, it sets up a form of dependency which involves the creation of a financial, educational, and social forms of control and these serve the needs of colonial administrators in the form of hidden agenda and cooptation. This dependency is administered on most reservations through numerous agencies of the federal government (Levitan and Johnson, 1975). Not only does the government hold title to the land on which reservation Indians live, but also have authority over nearly all forms of Indian affairs and this includes the educational system, the health services, welfare and social assistance. By establishing an agenda of dominance, the government has left the minor issues outside of their control and have called them tribal rights. These include the right to establish conditions for tribal membership, to choose their local forms of government, to levy taxes and regulate their own domestic relations, to set property law which does not conflict with federal ownership, and to administer justice as long as it does not threaten the balance of power.

Other rights available to Native Americans include the right to vote, but this was long overdue and came with the granting of citizenship rights in 1924. If this concession appears to be a benevolent one, this is not viewed as such by political analyists who see voting as merely a form of political symbolism by which the power elite maintains its illusion of democracy while operating an industrial oligarchy. Nevertheless, these alleged rights do not offset dominance and its establishment of a dominance relationship which works at the disadvantage of reservation Indians. This dependency can be seen in the Department of Agriculture with its expenditures for Farmers' Home Administration, Soil Conservation Service, Rural Electrification, and Stabilization and Conservation Services. It can bee seen in the Department of Commerce which administers business loans, oversees regional action planning, guides economic development, and controls the planning of businesses. They have imposed their capitalistic versions of success and judge Native Americans accordingly. The Department of Interior does geological surveys on reservations, heads the Bureau of Reclamation and oversees sport fishing and wildlife. As for the Bureau of Indian Affairs, it controls the development of resources, and is involved in the construction of irrigation systems and road construction. The educational systems are directed by regulation through the Johnson-O'Malley Act of 1934 and more recently through the Elementary and Secondary Education Act of 1965. The Department of Health, Education and Welfare is under the dominance of the federal government and oversees education in addition to being in control of the Office of Native American Programs. Hence, the among and scope of direct dependency as a form of control by the federal government is staggering.

Another case of internal colonialism which merits comment can be found in the apartheid policy of South Africa. In that country, there are four officially defined racial groups: The Africans, the Whites, the Coloreds, and the Indians. The first group was in occupation when the White settlers arrived from the Netherlands about three centuries ago. The Khoikhoi, or as they were pejoratively called "the Hottentots," were the original inhabitants of the Western Cape, but they were rapidly subjugated and became the servants of the new settlers. As slaves were imported from the Indias and other parts of Africa they came to form distinctive colored communities, but due to the rigid relationship of power and control they became objects of racial antagonism. The Indian population came much later and were brought in as indentured servants (Troup, 1976), and worked in the sugar plantations owned by British settlers. As they grew in number and became rivals in the economic system, they were denied their political rights and subjected to racial discrimination.

The effort to create social distance between the master and the slave took many forms. There were miscegenation laws which prohibited Black from marrying Whites and later this was extended to cover Coloreds. There were "pass laws" which required the working class to register themselves by means of passports. Many thousands of these people became victims of "influx control" and arrested daily in the process of an identity search. This separation was all part of the policy of Apartheid under the rule of the Nationalist Party which has ruled in South Africa for three decades. The basis of this "separate development" is not only socio-economic in nature, it is also political. The race of a people is used in classifying them and this determines where they may be permitted to live and where they are forced to work. Nowhere is this pattern of discrimination more readily apparent than in the educational system.

Although the development of the European model of education and can be traced back to 1658 in South Africa, its use for political socialization begins to emerge rather clearly under the Cape Education Act of 1865. This required that state aid be given to three types of schools: public, mission, and native schools. These schools reflected racial barriers. The mission schools were open to all races, but by the 1890s the department of education began to discourage Whites from attending and this was due to, in part, to the increase in colonialist pressures for segregation. By 1905, the Cape School Board Act established separate public schools where White children were prevented from being brought into daily contact with those of other races. With the take over of the Nationalist government in 1948, one of the first acts was to establish the principles and aims of education for Natives as an independent race. It was argued that Africans should receive an education which was tailored to their place within the system. This meant, of course, the training of a working class limited to labor and excluded from the more skilled occupations. As for the Whites, they were trained within a system of Christian National Education with its extreme Calvinist and Fundamentalist docture. They were taught that according to their religious doctrine they should be imbued with the love of one's own and this meant, in particular, the love of one's language, culture, and history. The key subject of the school, of course, was religion. It is God's will, they learned, that man should master the earth and rule over it. Education, then, enables the young to take over from their cultural heritage everything that was deemed good and beautiful and noble. And, they were to develop this heritage in accordance with their own gifts.

The content of the school system for these Christian Nationalists (not to be confused with the missionary schools supported by the non-legitimate churches and unofficial dogma) discouraged bilingualism. The nation was rooted in a country alloted to it by God (Troup, 1976:19). The Mother-tongue was the only medium of instruction and provided the basis for cultivating a sense of nationalism. As for the native schools, they had a different curriculum. In Article 15 of the manifesto of the Institute for Christian National Education of February 1948, it stated clearly that native education was based on the principles of trusteeship, non-equality, and segregation. Its aim was one of inculcating the White man's view of life of which he was the senior trustee. The natives, it was argued, were in a state of cultural infancy and it was the duty of the state to provide them with paternal guidance. In another article of the pamphlet of Christian Nationalist Education principles, it was argued and reiterated that the task of the White South African is to christianize the native and to help him culturally and in order to do this he must be grounded in the life and the world-view of the Whites who were the trustees of the natives within the Boer nation. Later, under the Bantu Education Act of 1953, it was emphasized that natives will be taught from childhood that they should not be considered equals with Europeans as there is no place for them in the European community above the level of certain forms of labor and servitude (Bunting, 1964).

The system of oppression has been well documented in

69

quantitative terms by Brian Bunting (1964), Freda Troup (1976) and others. However, when this is reassessed in terms of human suffering and negative self-concept, the acuity of the problem becomes readily understandable. N. C. Manganyi (1973) describes what it is like to be Black in the White world of South Africa. He discusses the concept of Black consciousness, the assault on Africa cultures resulting in a demise of historicity, and the dichotomy between "us" and "them". He comments on how the quest for purity is manifested in terms of reality maintenance by Whites who attempt to create an aura of sacredness around their ideology, and who have incorporated highly emotional lexemes into their language which reflect attitudes of racial control. They have defined themselves, for example, as "people" and for those who have no right of existence in their political and social world, they have labelled "non-people". This work is done within the existential tradition and portrays the feelings of anxiety and insecurity characteristically associated with racial oppression. In this sense, it is reminiscence of the works of Franz Fanon (1952; 1961) and Albert Memmi (1968) on Algeria, and the state of socio-economic and racial oppression felt by Blacks in the United States (Banks and Gramb, 1972).

LANGUAGE EDUCATION AND THE URBAN WORKING CLASS

Language is a significant factor in negotiating social reality and this is particularly evident in the situation where the mass culture has emerged from an industrial context into a life of cultural materialism and a consumer ethic. An insightful description of this process can be found in the research of Stuart Ewen (1977). He notes how the issue of social control within the history of industrial capitalism has revolved mainly around the question of work. For the large numbers of immigrants and minorities who went to the factories or served the wealthy before the turn of the century, work was synonymous with misery and income was equated with wage-slavery. This interpretation of the system by the masses required resocialization. The masses, it was argued, must be given a new sense of social reality. They are in need of a new kind of culture. They must learn to appreciate that time is money and that their lives must be synchronized to the mechanical rhythms of the factory. They must learn to view themselves as potential citizens in a new industrial civilization rather than as mere "wheelhorses" in the productive process. They need to learn how to inter-calate their work day with periods of play so that they can "re-create" themselves. In the language and civic classes of the immigrant, the orientation must be toward industrial discipline and a respect for the new social order. From the point of view of the power elite, social and educational pro-blems in language and education were clearly defined. The captains of industry were in the business of becoming cap-tains of consciousness.

The form of political socialization that Stuart Ewen describes in his research is advertising through the mass media. He discusses how advertisers were brought in to assist industry in changing the attitudes of the factory workers toward their jobs. In addition, at that time the mass produced goods were aimed at an elite market which was rapidly dwindling and it was through the use of advertising that new markets were created among the buying public. This massification of industry required that the worker should also become the consumer. When higher wages and shorter hours were granted to workers it was not because of the magnanimity of the financial moguls, but because it was believed that such a move would enhance mass consumption. The new priorities dictated that the worker spend more of his leisure time and hard earned wages as a consumer on the mass market. Social psychologists assisted in this process by studying how the use of value and emotion could incorporated into the "fancied needs" of the new popular culture. The use of these psychological methods were meant to turn the con-sumers away from the product and toward themselves. Their critical functions were not allowed to judge the intrinsic worth of the product. Buying was imbued with the illusions of status symbols and the mobilizing of instincts.

To enhance the creation of the new culture, advertisers worked closely with industry to Americanize the immigrant. They were told, for example, that it was un-American to repair things and that in this country one must learn how to discard old worn-out objects. The mania for "newness" became the motto of the industry. This political ideology of con-sumption was directly incorporated into the various "ethnic" newspapers of the times. Most immigrant presses in the country were owned and managed by advertising agencies. Consumerism became an aggressive device of corporate survival, and it did not limit itself to the print medium. It also began to effect the graphic and performing arts. Artistic creativity was constrained to the needs of consumerization. Artists were called upon to use their skills and talents for commercial manipulation.

Language was one of the dominant means of creating the illusion of happiness in education and advertising (Violas, 1978). After all the control of the masses required that these concumers enjoying the world in which they lived. Fantasy in film, art, and language became an intrinsic part of the new spectator culture. It created a feeling of euphoria that concealed the emptiness and anxiety of the market place. The populace was not schooled in the acquisition of mere literacy. What they needed, it was argued, was mass culture. They needed to learn to respect the corporate image, adapt to the technology of their machine civilization, view the buying process as one of voting for good products, and to treat work and wages in terms of careers or vocations.

CONCLUDING REMARKS

Since language is the medium of instruction and the basis for conveying commercial images in advertising, it provides an informative forum for the social, historical, and political analysis of agenda-setting within an order society. The case in which students from a foreign country are Americanized under the guise of language education is just one example of the process of political socialization. This same approach to educating one into the system can also be found the context of colonialism as well as in the training of the urban working class. This process of political socialization is important because it takes place in the public domain. It is public language. Where conflicts do occur, they result from differences between the various sectors of society. For the oppressed within a colonial system, it is their culture and their self-concept which is threatened. The new language brings with it new values and new demands. For the immigrant in a consumer-oriented society, the threat comes in the form of new beliefs and new anxieties which demand a readjustment of attitudes. The new language devalues the old and the new culture stigmatizes the heritage that one has. In these instances, language is directly involved in the processes of social change. It becomes a barometer for public behavior. There are times, however, when language plays a more neutral and ritualistic role. In a homogeneous society where social expectations tend to be communal, language acts to confirm one's reality and legitimize one's presence within the system. For many who utilize language as an instrument of political socialization, the goal is to have one culture, one belief system, and one shared concept of what is sacred and rewarding. Hence, in the context of biculturalism, language may play a cohesive role among ingroups and it may create social distances and redefine boundaries among outgroups. In either case, it is endemic to the process.

REFERENCES

Banks, James and Gramb, Jean D. Black Self-Concept: Implications for Education and Social Science. N.Y.: McGraw-Hill, 1972.

Basu, Aparna. Policy and Conflict in India: The Reality and Perception of Education. In Philip Altbach and Gail Kelly (Eds.), Education and Colonialism. N.Y.: Longman, 1978.

Bowles, Samuel and Gintis, Herbert. Schooling in Capitalist America: Educational Reform and The Contradiction of American Life. N.Y: Basic Books, 1976.

Bunting, Brian. The Rise of the South African Reich. Baltimore, MD.: Penguin Books, 1964.

Easton, David and Dennis, J. Children in the Political System: The Origin of Political Legitimation. N.Y.: McGraw-Hill, 1969.

Ewen, Stuart. Captains of Consciousness: Advertising and The Social Role of the Consumer Culture. N.Y.: McGraw-Hill, 1977.

Fanon, Franz. Peaux noires et masques blancs. Paris: Le Seuil, 1952.

Fanon, Franz. La fammes de la terre. Paris: Maspero, 1961.

Iverson, Katherine. Civilization and Assimilation: The Colonized Schooling of Native Americans. In Philip Altbach and Gail Kelly (Eds.), Education and Colonialism. N.Y.: Longman, 1978.

Jones, M. A. American Immigration. Chicago: University of Chicago Press, 1974.

Kelly, Gail. Colonized Schools in Vietnam: Policies and Practice. In Philip Altbach and Gail Kelly (Eds.), Education and Colonialism. N.Y.: Longman, 1978.

Levitan, Sar A. and Johnston, William B. Indian Giving: Federal Programs for Native Americans. Baltimore, Md.: The Johns Hopkins Press, 1975.

Manganyi, N.C. Being-Black-in-the-World. Johannesburg, South Africa: Ravan Press, 1973.

Memmi, Albert. L'homme dominé: Le noir - lé colonise - la femme - le prolétaire - le juif - le domestique. Paris: Pettite Biblioteque Payot, 1968.

Novotny, A. Strangers at the Door. N.Y.: Bantam Pathfinder, 1974.

Prewitt, Kenneth and Stone, Alan. The Ruling Elites: Elite Theory, Powers, and American Democracy. N.Y.: Harper and Row, 1973.

Thompson, F.V. Schooling and the Immigrant. Montclair, N.J.: Paterson Smith, 1971.

Troup, Freda. Forbidden Pastures: Education under Apartheid. London: International Defense and Aid Fund, 1976.

Violas, Paul. The Training of the Urban Working Class: A History of Twentieth Century American Education. Chicago: Rand McNally, 1978.

CHAPTER 5

BRITISH-TRADITION ENGLISH IN THE AMERICAN UNIVERSITY

Betty Lou Dubois
New Mexico State University

INTRODUCTION

As far as I know, the fate of British-tradition English in the universities of our country is not being studied or even discussed. I will therefore give an account, in a rather practical, ad hoc fashion, of my experience with students with long immersion in British English--not just those who have had a British teacher here and there or used British textbooks as they studied English as a foreign langauge-- during the pursuit of their education at a particular university with a particular set of conditions, attitudes and traditions, New Mexico State University. Perhaps after many such studies of British-tradition English at various sites, we will one day be able to discuss its status in the American university, instead of in an American university, as I will now do.

THE UNIVERSITY SETTING

New Mexico State University began its existence in 1889 as the New Mexico College of Agricultural and Mechanical Arts, a land grant institution. During perhaps the first fifty years of its existence, New Mexico A&M was a small school which devoted the major part of its efforts toward agriculture, as might be expected from the name. In the 1950's, during the Sputnik scare, attention was turned toward other sciences, resulting in the development of comparably good programs in pure and applied scientific fields. The Colleges of Education and Business Administration, like the previously mentioned fields, grew apace with overall university growth in the immediate post-World War II and subsequent periods. During most of the history of the institution, social sciences and liberal and fine arts functioned chiefly as service appendages to the scientific divisions, although recently, efforts are being made to bring the arts and the rest of the sciences into the prominence they must have if the University is to be truly deserving of the name.

It is no surprise that a university that has made an international reputation in agriculture and engineering should attract international student to study chiefly in those areas. Many administrators and faculty members from these disciplines have consulted in various countries of the world, and they have often been our most effective student recruiters. Visitors to the campus, as well as alumni, also help to attract students from other countries. It seems reasonable to say that at least 90% of our international students take degrees in agriculture, engineering, or one of the pure sciences. During the past three and a half years, a few have majored in economics or business administration, one in guidance, two in mass communications, a couple in education-- extension education at that!--and so on.

Not by accident, New Mexico State has a fair proportion of international students, not only because of offerings in specialities urgently desired by developing nations, but also because the university prides itself on its genuine commitment to international education. Besides the informal recruiting mentioned in the previous paragraph, the Office of International Programs actively seeks qualified students and oversees their welfare one they are here. Moreover, the commitment to international education extends from the administration to the faculty as well. With a few notable exceptions, faculty are genuinely dedicated to the education of such students and are on occasion willing to go far out of their ordinary routines to offer needed help. It is not at all unusual to find a faculty member giving a foreign student extra time to take an exam, substituting an oral exam for a student whose writing skills are not yet up to par, or carefully regularizing the English on a student's term paper. Probably the size of the university--approximately 10,000 students on the main campus--is a factor in creating such a good climate for international students. Although the faculty is too large for some purposes, it has still not grown so much that interdepartment and intercollege communication has become difficult. It is easy to get to know concerned faculty across the campus to discuss problems which arise. Many called me for assistance and advice, and I feel free to reciprocate. In summary: although conditions for international students at New Mexico State University cannot be described as perfect, a supportive environment is created for them, far better, certainly, than at many other schools.

STUDENT ENGLISH BACKGROUND

The students in question arrive as more or less proficient speakers of what can be called transplanted English. Historically, transplantations of English have had three classes of result. When, as in the case of Australia, for example, sufficient speakers of English arrived in a new land, made their permanent homes there, bred in large enough numbers to establish themselves, the transplant "took" to the extent that English became fully established as a geographical variety, often swamping indigenous languages and later arrivals. In a second category of transplantation, for example, Jamaica, English in some sense established itself with the original inhabitants but in a wide range of varieties, from creole to standard; that is, language contact had very great effects on English. In the third type, English was brought not so much by settlers as by administrators and military men, who came in insufficient numbers to eradicate the preexisting languages of the territories. English therefore became a superposed governmental/administrative language which added to an already complex linguistic situation. Prime examples of the third transplant result are found in the Indian subcontinent and the former West African colonies of England.

Although the Indian subcontinent and West Africa bear some historical similarities in the establishment of English within their borders, there are still some differences. Kirk Greene points out that the British were in India for three hundred years; they arrived in West Africa a scant hundred years ago. In both cases, they met a language situation of enormous complexity, as measured in numbers of indigenous languages, but India, as opposed to the West African nations, had a history of written scholarship and high culture more than 2000 years ago. Sanskrit and Tamil were languages considered worthy of cultivation and study in

78

East and West alike. Moreover, India had at least one language of wider communication spoken by millions of people, a
condition not duplicated in West Africa. Finally, West
Africa--for good or ill-lacked groups of "indigenous British"
who identified their personal fate with that of the country,
as each region in which it has been transplanted would
require an extensive account of particular historical facts.
For purposes of the present paper, however, experience has
shown that there are actual similarities (and theoretical
considerations, to be discussed below) so that language
products of the third transplant situation can indeed be
treated as a single category. For simplicity, then, I will
deal with West Africa, students and assume that what is said
applies as well to East Africans, Indians, Pakistanis, and so
on.

To the question of what kind of English we are talking
about, no one can give a simple answer. As put succintly by
Spencer: "The West Africans who know and use English do not
constitute a homogeneous speech community in regard either to
their mother tongues or to English" (1971:7). School and
church offer consistent exposure to the most standard
English--formal written and spoken--that West Africans are
likely to encounter. Depending on topic and other factors,
business and governmental affairs may very likely be carried
on in English, although one more remote from British norms.
In the streets and in the play yards, it is possible to encounter pidgin, and on the coast and in certain urban
centers, creole. With such a spectrum of varieties, Spencer
warns against thinking of them as wholly separate, well-
defined, stressing the interpermeability of the varieties of
English to be found in West Africa.

Not only is there great variability present already
(which has recently been augmented by the presence of Peace
Corps teachers and the use of American T.V. programs), but
there is ongoing social change as well, with the result that:
"The place of English within the West African total language
configuration is not therefore static, nor are the attitudes
of their people toward English constant" (Spencer, 1971:1).
The position, function, prestige, and value of English
compared to indigenous languages is neither uniform nor
predictable from region, class, or educational background
(Banjo 1973:306). Because nearly all English-speaking West
Africans have English as a second language and retain their

79

maternal tongues, and because some have in addition an African language of wider communication, West Africans lack a full range of English styles and registers such as are necessary for British and Americans. For example, the choice of langue in away-from-home exchanges between adults can be influenced by a shared material language or an African language or wider communication. In the north of Nigeria, if there is no common native language, such conversations are customarily conducted in Hausa, but in the south, English is used (Kirk Greene 1971:128).

Amidst uncertainties about the status and kinds of English in West Africa, there is nevertheless evidence of the existence of a separate variety (or varieties): positive evidence in that, as Boadi has noted, many feel it "desirable for educated Ghanian users of English to impress their African personality on the language"; negative evidence in that others insist that a borrowed language had better be used "properly," (1971:53) a tacit admission of differences from British English. We are undoubtedly in presence of a widely-recognized phenomenon of prolonged language contact: "errors" in English have gradually become entrenched and widely used, with the resulting establishment of bilingual or contact norms. Dispute over the kind of English appropriate to West Africa will assuredly prove moot, since it it unimaginable that Africans can be made into speakers of perfectly British English even if they choose to accept the change. In fact, there already exists a serious literature-- both prose and poetry--West Africa and a thriving pot-boiler industry of prose romances, the Anitsha novelettes, which will help to establish the independence of the writer's African English.

What is wanted, clearly, is extensive descriptive study of the English used in the region, to identify existent/ nascent dialect(s). Despite the present lack of such work, it is possible to characterize, however tentatively, the English of some West Africans as possessing some or all of the following (Spencer 1971:26-29):

1. Syllable timing
2. Tonicity
3. Narrow range of syllable structures
   (resulting from cluster
   simplification)

4. Reduction of vowel contrasts
5. Loss of postvocalic nasal consonants
   (realization with previous vowel)
6. Simplified inflectional system
7. Vocabularly differences with British
   English (variant collocation, retention
   of older meanings, rule generalization,
   borrowed and coined words, etc.).

NMSU ENGLISH PROGRAM

Courses

The English program for international students at NMSU
came into existence as a direct response to the needs of
students, as evidenced by complaints from the faculty and
academic failures. Very few international students succeeded
in the normal freshman English composition class in com-
petition with American students; a three-hour composition
course was set up, therefore, to substitute for it. While
three hours of composition (with a heavy dose of reading,
speaking, and selected advanced grammar topics) is sufficient
for a portion of the students, others arrive needing more
extensive grammar review and practice in speaking. Those
from countries where English is a foreign rather than a
second language and where Neolithic language teaching is
still the rule can arrive with a very low level of English
proficiency indeed, if we define proficiency as "ability to
receive or transmit information in the...language for some
pragmatically useful purpose within a real-life setting"
(Clark 1975:10).

After study which has consisted of grammatical analysis
and translation, they are essentially unable to speak,
understand, read, or write. For these students, three pre-
liminary courses were added to the curriculum. The first two
constitute a one-year elementary sequence to which students
having a TOEFL score of 350 or below are to be assigned.
Because of inadequate staffing, they have never been offered,
to my knowledge. The third, given every semester, is an
intermediate grammar review with emphasis on speaking, which
originally met five hours per week for three hours credit--

since intermediate courses in other languages carry full credit--has relieved the situation.

Admission of Students

Students regularly admitted to the University who do not have U.S. citizenship and who apply directly from a foreign country have in theory been required to submit a TOEFL (Test of English as a Foreign Language) based on our past experience with their countrymen here. There has apparently been no rigidly fixed minimum admission score, but something in the neighborhood of 425 is considered acceptable, except that 450 is required for students from certain countries who, in the main, have demonstrated little interest in improving their English skills and who thus need a higher beginning level. In previous semesters, various exceptions were made for particular students. In addition, West Africans have been routinely admitted without examination, given that their secondary schooling has been in English and that at least in school, they have been functioning effectively in English for several years. Numbers of international students admitted to our university have increased dramatically in the past two years--catastrophically for the teaching staff--it would be easy to double the number again. However, because of dissatisfaction with the performance of a portion of the students and because a substantial increase in servicing the English program is not high on the University priority list, the Faculty Senate has recently passed a bill requiring a 500 TOEFL score for admission, a policy to be applied uniformly to all students, regardless of their country of origin or whether they are graduates or undergraduates.

Other routes of admission are open. A student who has studied English at an accredited university is of course given transfer credit although some of them are not minimally proficient by NMSU standards. A student who has graduated from a U.S. high school is admitted without being required to demonstrate English proficiency. Such students are comparatively rare; the few we have have shown themselves to be quite proficient. Any person--regardless of previous education or language skill--can be admitted to nondegree status through the College of Continuing Education and can enroll in any course offered. The students who came into the English program via this route have been mainly student wives or recent immigrants without previous formal study of English. They should obviously be in a beginning course, but since there is none, they are accepted into the intermediate one, although they cannot meet the requirements in one or even two semesters. An occasional international student who intends to become a degree candidate enters the university through this backdoor route. If large numbers become aware of this possibility, a special policy may have to be adopted to cover the situation.

Placement

Having only two courses and having made the decision not to refuse admission to the lower one to underprepared students (they are, however, warned that they may not be able to meet the requirements in one semester). NMSU has three placement possibilities: 103 (the intermediate course), 104 (the alternate freshman composition course), and exemption from further study. The placement procedure in operation when I came in January 1973 was intermediate between an informal system such as the one then in operation at the University of New Mexico (if possible, students were enrolled in one of the three courses according to evaluation of transcripts; the residue were enrolled in the beginning course, to be sorted out on the basis of the first week's performance) and an elaborate, fully normal system such as that of the University of Michigan or UCLA. At NMSU, the Michigan Test of English Language Proficiency (less the oral and composition sections) was administered to all incoming students and placement was done according to cutoff points determined from actual experience. In general, cutoffs were lower than the recommendation listed in the accompanying Manual, and in no case was a student's total academic load reduced.

Then, as now, the instructor had authority to rectify placement errors on the basis of performance at the beginning of the semester, and serious efforts was (and is) made to verify placement. Reasons for shifting downward include lack of speaking ability to match test scores and lack of writing ability, i.e., inability achieve functional integration of the discrete points tested by the Michigan instrument. Reasons for shifting upward include the usual questions of test reliability (an occasional student has a bad day caused by jet lag, is relatively unfamiliar with multiple choice exams with separate answer sheets, or has little experience with speeded exams) and dialect and style matters. Students who use West African English fluently may show up poorly on the Michigan Test, which emphasizes formal written American English norms. Incidentally, the same is true for some native New Mexicans, university seniors ready to graduate who scores would place them in a class of English language study with reduced academic classload, if the Michigan placement recommendations were followed. In fairness to the Michigan Test, let me state that it makes no claim to validity other than for those for whom English is truly a foreign language.

The Michigan Test has been retained as our initial placement tool because it has worked well in the circumstances. Our English program is small--next fall there will be three sections taught one by me and two by another staff member--and we have not only a great deal of administrative flexibility, but cooperation from concerned academic departments and administrators. The other side of the coin is that our small size is a disadvantage in that, if we had a large number of international students, we might set aside a class exclusively for West Africans and pitch it to their proficiency levels.

COMPARISON TO SPANISH FOR THE SPANISH-SPEAKING

Enough has been written to show that there are certain similarities in the situation described to that of the Spanish-speaking in the United States who for administrative reasons must be put in foreign language Spanish classes. At the early stages, such an arrangement makes rational materials selection impossible. Beginners are willing to work with a foreign language textbook containing exercises, but I have not found West Africans willing to do so. It must be the case also with the Spanish-speaking, for it is insulting to proficient speakers to ask them to use materials far below their level. I have my greatest success with West Africans using newspapers, magazines and a novel as textbooks. Even when the materials are suitable, however, West African and Spanish speakers alike most often find them written in a dialect not their own. Probably West Africans

84

have an easier time of it than Chicanos, for example, being long accustomed to decoding into their dialects. The two groups may share an unwillingness to adopt the dialect used by the instructional staff, if it is already not their own. The customary dialect serves as vehicle for personal and social identity, which few of us are willing to renounce. Moreover, adopting the classroom dialect may involve more or less conscious identification with another country: for Chicanos, with Mexico, if the northern dialect of that country is being used; for West Africans, with the United States, while their previous English loyalty has been toward Britian.

There are also marked differences between the two groups. The West African students represent the top products of their countries' educational systems. They are adventuresome, adaptable, ambitious. They are aware of the need back home for education, and many come genuinely dedicated to learning what they can to help their countries when they return. Many have left government jobs to come to school and count upon a promotion when they have their degrees in hand. As to their social class, it is difficult for me to judge. I remember one young man's reply to a request to imagine his home at six p.m. and describe what is going on. He began: "We are sitting down waiting for dinner. The cook is preparing the meal, the houseboys are setting the table...." Others come from less urban, more traditional tribal settings, but all seem to have the feeling of upward personal mobility. They appear to take pride in their ability in English, which I judge a necessary though perhaps not a sufficient precondition for success.

It would be foolish and insulting to describe Chicanos merely as the opposite of West African students, for both groups partake of the range of human intelligence and traits. Yet, the situation of Chicanos as a largely lower socio-economic, racially indentifiable, linguistic minority has had its adverse effect. Chicanos are not so confident of being able to find a useful, satisfying occupation. Not only are they not their country's top educational products, they are in fact, as a group, systematically excluded from the higher reaches of the educational system. They are not always the eager, self-assured learners that the West Africans students mainly are, but I have no doubt that Spanish language courses designed to capitalize on their abilities--both receptive and productive--and to teach them what they need to know will accomplish a great deal in this direction. Contrary to West Africans, until recently they have not been encouraged to be proud of their Spanish and in fact among educators the question of the use of Southwestern Spanish is still keenly debated.

SPECIAL NEEDS OF WEST AFRICANS

All students, including American citizens, who came to the University need to learn to read better, to expand their vocabularies, to use the words they alread know with greater precision and art, to express themselves effectively in speaking and writing. West African students, who arrive relatively proficient in English, have further needs, two of which, I am sure, they do not willingly recognize. The first is for greater intelligibility in speech, apparently not a problem in the home countries. Some of the sound features to be found in West African English are listed earlier; all of them are in evidence of NMSU students.

In addition to syllable timing, cluster simplification, and tonicity, I have found phoneme substitution, for example, /f/ for initial /p/, /v/ and /b/ confusion, /s/ for /θ/ and so on. Reduction of vowel contrasts is quite obvious. All students I have encountered are r-less which causes no difficutly here, since some Americans are r-less too. H-dropping is prevalent, again without affecting intelligiblity. Interestingly enough, been and being, seen and seeing have become homonyms, as indeeds the latter pair are for at least some Americans. Post-vocalic /n/ is realized most often as a nasal, although for some students it has disappeared, i.e., /kant/. The latter was a little hard for me to learn to understand, but in general, individual phoneme errors cause a little problem in intelligibility, as the listener can adapt readily. What cannot so easily be compensated for is syllable timing and tonicity, which seriously compromise intelligibility of speech, especially for university personnel not accustomed to dealing with international students.

I have attempted to work on these problems in class through modified TESOL techniques (little success) and out of class by having selected students use an excellent set of pronunciation tapes under unsupervised conditions (little success). We have the possibility of using new laboratory facilities and I am sure that it will be worth a try to self-pace the pronunciation course and hold out the reward of early release upon completion of reasonable objectives. Meanwhile, much of the work in both English courses is done in small groups. I make certain that the groups contain students from various language groups and in these groups at least, the West Africans must make themselves clearly understood.

Intelligibility of writing presents another sort of problem, one which is equally difficult to attack. Some, though certainly not all, students' writing seems diffuse, elusive in meaning. More words are used than seem necessary, and many are used in ways so remote from American norms that it is difficult to construe sentences precisely. A few samples will illustrate.

> Before Laughing Boy and Slim Girl had planned to return to the people, everyone of them had understood each other. They very much more improved their love and every one had believed that one could not nicely survive without the other, and probed that any where they go they would settle in a good and peaceful condition.

> An individual of this norm lives a physical and harmonious mental relaxation with every member of his group. Unstable as she is with no ego-culture bounds, she joined this new dehumanizing prostitution and made a better and probably endless just for profit enterprise.

> Slim girl was not unlucky as culturally deprived. These people also translated her civilization as a cost of culture and respect for their traditions.

> I hope that one day I will be back to
> Nigeria and for some the first week will
> be of difference to my people.

This phenomenon may be no more than a result of inexperience and undereducation in English, some of it at the
hands of teachers not fully proficient themselves. Bowen
(1973:299) notes, for example, the disastrous effect of the
Kenya system, where English was taught in rural elementary
schools by teachers inadequately prepared and supervised.
(Additional evidence of undereducation can be found in West
African spelling pronunciation, for example, /klowdiz/
/klowdz/. Undereducation is, of course, found in native
speakers of English; if they happen to be university students
and it is manifested in vocabulary, we call it "collegese."
The following sample, from a U.S. born Chicano, shows the
same kind of diffuse vocabulary usage, I think:

> Leaving the Cd. Juarez city limits, one
> is immediately struck with the pride of
> being an international citizen because of
> the primordial traits that the Mexicans
> and the Mexican-Americans share. The
> countryside along the road to Chihuahua
> almost declames the bloody history that
> took place there and instead, one sees a
> resplendent countryside of bucolic
> serenity.

Such writing is of course not the monopoly of Chicanos,
for many monolingual English speakers write that way, too. A
complicating factor, one which makes it risky to dismiss such
West African writing as the result entirely of inexperience
and undereducation, is the presence of published popular
fiction which displays the same characteristics. Kirk Greene
(1971:130, 132) gives examples from the Onitsha novelettes:

> ....they look out for flimsy excuses to
> issue you queries. It is known to my
> poorself the hows and whys of politics.
> As from now I shall group of politicians-
> -peoples of varied wishes that assume one
> name. Politics is forced out tears by
> intense anger. One can not remember any
> time both in dream and normal life that

> poorself stood among honourable ones,
> expressing in opposition terms against a
> number more than one, of course, except
> in concerts.

This writing may perhaps be an illustration of established semantic differences from British English which Banjo (1973:307) says are the most notable characteristic of African English. A second major need of West Africans, at least as far as their stay in the United States is concerned, is for the full inflectional systems of English. Typical of the reduction to be found are the following two examples:

> ...Slim Girl [s] inability to bear
> children...

> ...If they succeeded in returning to the
> people.

The absence of a grammatical morpheme does not often affect intelligibility greatly, all other things being equal, but I fear that some Americans associate reduced inflection with poverty and ignorance, even stupidity, the more so when the speaker's skin is dark. I am convinced that absence of inflection can produce emotional barriers to communication and at a minimum bad attitudinal side effects. A solution, however, is difficult to find. West African students seem, as a whole, quite indifferent to standarizing their English morphology, for reasons discussed above. Second language teaching techniques most emphatically do not work for this group, at least in any way in which I have used them myself. To the contrary, most Africans refuse to participate at all.

Reduction in the number of vowel contrasts in the English of West Africans shows up in their writing, too. Sometimes it causes very little miscommunication, as in the following sentence: "Their love will stand the taste of time." The only genuine collocational possibility for the cliche is _test_. One can also quickly accommodate to _human been_ instead of _human being_. Sometimes, however, I am brought up short, as the day when I read something on the order of "the truth of their situation licked out." Asked to explain, the student informed me that _lick out_ is very common Nigeria, and I was about to store this very vivid metaphor in my mind when I realized that he intended _leak out_. The absence of /h/, postvocalic /n/, and /r/ causes another order of writing difficult. Sometimes one will be omitted, as tied for tired; sometimes one will be added, as heat for eat, confindent instead of confident. Since West African pronunciation makes the spelling of a large number of such words a less faithful rendering than mine does, for example, they have to memorize a greater number of words than I have as containing silent letters (as gnome and thumb do speakers of all dialects).

The concerns just listed are headed "Special Needs of West Africans," but they have proved to be quite general ones. The question arises whether the needs ought to be diagnosed in a more systematic fashion, by the use of contrastive analysis. It would be pointless to rehearse the contrastive analysis-error analysis controversy here, and I have already taken my stand against contrastive analysis (Dubois and Fallis n.d.). It is fortunate for me that I arrived at this point of view, for doing contrastive analyses of English and West African languages would be a practical impossibility, beyond a rudimentary matching up of lists of phonemes. Regardless of questions of definition of language and dialect, the language situation of the region is enormously complicated. Ayo (1971:36) says there are four hundred local languages in Nigeria; Boadi (1971:49) claims forty for Ghana. Moreover--and this to me the most compelling reason for rejecting the contrastive analysis hypothesis--one can maintain the illusion that errors in a target language are the product of "interference" from the first language only so long as blinkers confine one to those two languages. In classes such as those at NMSU, with students of many language backgrounds, it is easy to see that the first language is not a determining factor for student, morphological errors. For example, West African English was earlier claimed to be inflectionally simplified, which is certainly the case in the English of the students at NMSU. However, the same inflectional simplification is found in the English of speakers of Spanish and of Chinese, the one more inflected than English, the other far less. How, in these circumstances, can we say that either language is the "cause" of morpheme reduction in learner English? This is the theoretical consideration, mentioned much earlier, which enables me to deal with Indians and Nigerians as a group, attacking their errors as they appear.

SOCIAL AND EDUCATIONAL ISSUES

A third need for for a greater sociolingustic range than West Africans bring them, specifically, the rules for speaking with their American counterparts. One of the fundamental purposes of international education is people-to-people interchange, and international students must learn how to approach their contemporaries. Second, a natural laboratory for increasing intelligibility is free, natural conversation with peers. A third reason concerns the social life of the West Africans. A few of the young men have wives with them, and the others feel the need for female companionship. Some succeed in dating American women almost immediately, but for most, disappointment is in store. What is involved is, of course, a deep-seated attitude toward women (in addition to sociolinguistic rules), and few of our young women are prepared to accept the dominating attitudes of West Africans. Another factor which comes into play is the rather conservative nature of our student population. My guess is that we have a smaller percentage of young women ready to accept the companionship of international students, particularly dark-skinned ones, than huge metropolitan schools do. Unfortunately, however much of the students' personal lives would be enriched by a broader range of sociolinguistic skills, such cannot be the main goal of the University TESOL classes. "In teaching English to foreign students at the university level, we have been recognizing that our instruction falls short of their need. We have been leaving them inadequately equipped with the skills they need for coping with university-level instruction in English. The need is for earlier and stronger emphasis on reading processes, and for teaching the more formal style required by textbooks and lectures rather than the conversational style of the Audio/Lingual materials" (Saville-Troike 1975:1).

Proficiency objectives for the two NMSU course have for two years been written in terms of the formal English--formal speaking, formal writing, formal information exchange--that is required in university classrooms. As time allows, I show informal equivalents and discussion relations with American university students as questions arise, but incresing the sociolingustic range in this direction unfortunately cannot be the main priority of the program.

91

REFERENCES

Ayo, Bamgbose. 1971. "The English Language in Nigeria." In Spencer 1971.

Banjo, Ayo. 1973. "Review of Spencer 1971." Language in Society. 2(2): 303-308.

Boadi, L. A. 1971. "Education and the Role of English in Ghana." In Spencer 1971.

Bowen, J. Donald. 1973. Rev. of Julian Dakin, Brian Tiffin, and H. G. Widdowson. Language in Education: The Problem in Africa and the Indo-Pakistan Sub-Continent. Language in Society. 2(2):298-300.

Clark, John L. D. 1975. "Theoretical and Technical Considerations in Oral Proficiency Testing." In Randall L. L. Jones and Bernard Spolsky, eds. Testing Language Proficiency. Arlington: Center for Applied Linguistics.

Dubois, Betty Lou, and Gradalupe Valdés-Fallis. "Mexican-American Child Bilingualism: Double Deficit?" ERIC ED 108 463. Rev. version accepted for a book of readings edited by Walburga von Raffler-Engel. ERIC/CRESS ED 104 595.

Kirk, Greene. 1971. "The Influence of West African Languages on English." In Spencer 1971.

Saville-Troike, Muriel. 1974. "TESOL Today". The Need for New Direction TESOL Newsletter. 7(5 & 6):1-2, 6.

Spencer, John, ed. 1971. The English Language in West Africa. London: Longman.

CHAPTER 6

TEACHING STANDARD VERSUS NON-STANDARD SPANISH

IN A STUDY ABROAD PROGRAM

Anthony Girard Lozano
University of Colorado

The question of teaching a standard dialect to Chicano students who are studying abroad has implications for teaching any standard versus non-standard dialect at other locations. The University of Colorado has a program at the Universidad Veracruzana in Jalapa, México. In this city the Chicano student is faced with standard Spanish, Chicano Spanish, elementary or near-standard Spanish spoken by Anglo students, and local non-standard Spanish. The policy which is followed within the program is to teach standard Spanish as an additional dialect to those students who already speak Chicano Spanish. The policy is made clear both to the students in the program as well as the Mexican professors who teach the language classes. In the Spring terms about one-half of the 62 students were Chicanos. The Chicano students demonstrated proficiency in Spanish ranging from fluent standard or Colorado Spanish to virtually no Spanish. An additional problem involved students who were compound bilinguals. In their case, one of the first objectives was to teach them the separation of their two languages. This, of course, involved an additional variety of language usage. Students who had a command of Spanish demonstrated language variation as shown by Mary Elizabeth Floyd in Verb Usage and Language Variation in Colorado Spanish. Different abilities in Spanish ranging from very fluent to non-existent should come as no surprise. The southwest is complex, both geographically and socially. It is a misconception to believe that a rigid monolithic dialect is spoken all over the southwestern United States. The fact of the matter is that various dialects and variations of Spanish are found throughout this region.

Valdés Fallis (1976b) examines three alternatives for teaching Spanish to Spanish speakers including: (1) erradication approach, (2) biloquialism and (3) appreciation

93

of dialect differences.   We agree with her that the second
alternative, the same as our "additonal dialect," is the most
advantageous approach.   She, however, goes on to point out
that, "we may have to admit that we are simply eradicators in
disguise and that we do believe that there is a right and a
wrong kind of Spanish."   (22).   Since a biloguial approach
can be coupled with the preparation of teachers in the
characteristics of local Spanish, we have at least dealt with
the bulk of material including the standard and local
varieties of Spanish. Since the choice will ultimately be up
to the individual, we are not dictating that he will use
standard Spanish in the barrio nor are we requiring him to
use local Spanish in a formal situation.

     Valdés Fallis (1976b: 20-21) mentions the disagreement
among scholars as to whether or not a second dialect can be
taught.   An individual manipulates a number of varieties of
the same language ranging from formal to intimate usage and
may include various languages if he is a bilingual or multilingual speaker.   Because of this ability to manipulate
various types within the same language and various languages,
the acquisition of a second dialect is very plausible.   If it
can be acquired it can be taught.   The use of different
varieties of Spanish by the same individuals was demonstrated
by the undersigned (1964) in a study of spoken styles in
Colombian Spanish.

     Nasario Garcia (1976) attempts to justify the teaching
of standard Spanish while using "sub-standard" Spanish as a
means for acquiring the standard.   Nevertheless, the tone of
his article is defensive in seeming to be apologetic about
local Spanish and appearing critical of Chicano teachers and
aides who reject the use of standard Spanish.   His label of
"sub standard" is ill chosen since it relegates the local
variety of Spanish to a secondary status.   The ultimate decision of using the local dialect or a standard will not be
made by the teacher but by the individual.   By following a
policy of teaching a standard dialect as an alternative, the
choice is still left to the individual although he is
required to practice standard forms during his formal course
work.   The argument concerning standard versus non-standard
is overly simplified since it does not take into account the
many possibilities of language variation typical of the
Southwest.   As a case in point, a compound bilingual who is

94

dominant in English could be taught standard Spanish which, if he so chose, could then be used as the basis for learning his local variety of Spanish. It is pointless to argue the merits of teaching one variety of Spanish versus another. A solution satisfactory to both camps needs to be found and teaching the standard as an alternative seems to meet this need while the preparation of teachers can include a study of United States Spanish. The works listed in the bibliography by Teschner, Bills and Craddock (1975) can serve as the basis for presenting the characteristics of local varieties of Spanish to teachers and specialists in bilingual education.

Anderson addresses himself to the role of the teacher in a bilingual community and also argues (929) in favor of a bi-dialectical ability. Referring to teachers, he says, "if we are not bilingual and/or bidialectical we must have acquired by direct contact or reading or both an understanding of, and full responsibility for, the local forms of the language and of intentions of speaking it." As can be seen from the above, there are strong arguments in favor of a biloquial model.

Anderson goes on to discuss the teaching of reading to non-English speaking children. He argues the concept of using the home language to teach reading. The pedagogical problems involving reading and writing by Chicano university students are of a different type. We are faced with students who have had 12 years of schooling in English and virtually no preparation in literate skills. In other words, we are asked to teach formal composition to a student who speaks Spanish but is illiterate to a lesser or greater degree in this language. The teaching techniques which have to be developed for such an individual who is already literate in English of necessity must be different from teaching literate skills to a bilingual child.

Taking standard Spanish to mean the cultivated norm of Mexico City, how do we teach this as an additional dialect? One technique to establish the standard language as an alternative is to provide written exercises which develop the reading and writing skills of those students fluent in Colorado Spanish. As has been shown by Ross (1975) and Floyd (1976) the grammatical patterns at the command of Colorado speakers closely resemble syntactic patterns found in Mexican

Spanish. If we can make broad generalizatons about two
dialects so complex in their structures and social character-
izations we would have to say that the main differences between this dialect and standard Mexican Spanish would appear
to lie in different pronunciations of the same lexical items
and in the use of different lexical items for the same
concept. Pronunciation differences can be seen in entriega
(Colorado) vs. entraga (standard). Turning to the lexical
examples guajolote (standard vs. ganso (Colorado) both refer
to a turkey. Although the syntactic patterns of Colordo
Spanish and Mexican Spanish are similar, there are certain
recurring syntactic patterns in Colorado Spanish which can be
termed either non-standard forms, calques based on English,
or anomalous forms. As is universal in dialect studies,
these appear to be less in number than local pronunciations
or local lexical usages. Since they do appear to be less in
number, one could develop a program to emphasize the equivalent syntactic patterns in standard Spanish. For example,
the subjunctive of doubt in both Ross's and Floyd's studies
appears to be absent or infrequent in this dialect.
Exercises could be developed to teach this construction. In
free composition special attention can be paid to this syntactic pattern or other syntactic patterns which are infrequent in Colorado Spanish. In the composition class held
in Jalapa, three days a week were devoted to different types
of exercises. On Monday students were given dictations, thus
developing the writing skill of a selected passage which the
student then had to write. In addition, another type of
exercise was also presented on Mondays. These were called
"proof reading" exercises (correction de pruebas). This
involved a mimeographed page filled with different types of
errors. The errors, having been selected by the instructor
and inserted into the text, could range from spelling
mistakes to lexical mistakes to syntactic mistakes or to
calques. In fact, any type of mistake can be incorporated
into such an exercise. Thus, for a particular class needing
more practice in spelling, a set of materials could be
developed, concentrating on spelling mistakes. The advantage
of such exercises is in the economy of time and the concen-
tration on given types of errors within a paragraph or longer
passage. These exercises were given as home assignments
which were then presented and corrected in class by each
student. Since this requires less correction of each
exercise by the professor, the time saved can be used for

other activities. Furthermore, since the last stage of formal writing involves proofreading, the student is led to develop his skills in this final stage.

On Wednesdays the students were required to submit a two-page composition, original in content. These were submitted in notebooks in order to maintain control over the progress of the individual. Thus, by maintaining control of these notebooks the instructor could note if a student consistently made the same sort of syntactic mistakes in the first and second weeks. If so, he was given exercises in the third week on this particular syntactic pattern. Having received a translation exercise during the previous lecture, students present the translation exercise during the previous lecture, students present the translation in Spanish to class on Friday. These Friday translations were original Spanish passages, ranging in length from a paragraph to a page, translated into English. The student was then required to translate the exercise back from English into Spanish. The advantage in having a translation exercise of this type is that all of the students are required to do the translation within the limits of the grammar and vocabulary delimited by the orignal work. No translation, obviously, will be the same, but there will be some similarities. Once the translations have been corrected and discussed in class they can be compared with the original text in Spanish.

It was enlightening for the students to see the style and artistic techniques of a good writer. Alternative translations which do not occur during the exercise became evident upon examination of the original text. This constant writing over a period of four months with careful attention to given types of errors as well as instilling the discipline of frequent practice and the meeting of deadlines produced a marked improvement in writing skills.

Let us now examine four short passages chosen from a set of compositions. In order to compare each of the following passages written by a Chicano in the most advanced group, to an underlying passage in standard Spanish, we will speak "features" of the orignal passages. This term refers, then, to non-standard usages in order to avoid using the negative "errors" or mistakes." Many of the features of the following passages include particular prepositions and spellings.

Characteristics of Colorado Spanish are <u>piensaba, pien-samientos, tienanian</u> and <u>aparecidas</u>. Only one-standard use of gender was found: <u>ninguna concepción</u>. The choice of prepositions was based on English calques: <u>escribir de</u> (to write about), <u>la semajanza ellos tiene a</u> (the similarity they have to), <u>me vestí enropa caliente</u> (I dressed in warm clothes). Other syntactic features particular to the dialect of this Chicano student only include <u>me recordé</u> rather than <u>recordé</u> and no <u>más se tenía que ir al supermercado</u>. False cognates can be found in <u>concepciones</u> and <u>paradiso</u>. With respect to the English calques and false cognates, these features are obviously common to both the Chicano speaker and to English speaking students learning Spanish as a foreign language. Notice that passages adhere closely to the major syntactic characteristics of Mexican Spanish. These passages are selected from a list of compositions.

First Composition

<u>Par</u>[1] mí, debe ser facíl escribir <u>de</u>[2] mi familia mexicana porque la caracterésticas que me has impresionado más de todo es la semejanza que tienen <u>a</u>[3] mis padres (y)[4] partenla.

Sus costumbres culturales son muy <u>aparecidas</u>[5] a los de mis padres. En esto pueden ver <u>los</u>[6] <u>contribuciones</u>[7] que mi herencia mexicana ha hecho en mi vída a causa de ser nacido de mis padres, queines <u>tienián</u>[8] una herencia mas fuerte. Al vivir con mis señores ha servido para reforzar mi herencia porque antes (yo)[9] no la miraba <u>asimismo</u>.[10]

Second Composition

Antes de venir a México <u>piensaba</u>[1] que no tenia <u>ninguana</u>[2] <u>concepcion</u>[3] del país y su gente. <u>Ahí</u>[4] mis <u>piensamientos</u>[5] si han cambiado en estas tres semanas en México. Sí tenía <u>concepciones</u>,[6] ahora sé que poco sabia.

Muchos Mexicanos me preguntan, "Que peinsas de México?" Es muy dificíl contestar esa pregunta. Yo no estoy seguro de mis <u>piensamientos</u>.[8] Ahora no más comienzo a acostumbrarme a este país tan diferente al mío.

De seguro no esperaba una cultura tan diferente.

Cuando amanecí esa maña no había nada para comer en la casa. Ni vista[1] de David, mi hermanito quien estaba encargado de cocinar e ir de compras. Luego (me)[2] recordé que junto con su novia iba a assitir[3] a un casamiento todo el fin de semana.

Tabien me habia dicho que dejaria diez dolares encima del escritorio. Pues bien, si habia monedo ahi no más se[4] tenía que ir al supermercado.

A causa que hacía frio, me vestí en[5] ropa caliente, empuje mi motocicleta de las sala, la monté y sali a la calle.

Ninth Composition

Siempra me habían dicho que las Filipinas eran islas bellas, un paradiso[1] tropical. Que[2] desilusión a[3] enfrentarme con cinco días de lluvia sin paro.[4] No servia de[5] salir del ambiente tan aburrido del cuartel, la lluvia fortalezaba[6] la calidad de gris de mi depresion. Me sentia como que[7] habia pasado años lo mismos que un vago, viajendo de puerto a puerto, nunca encontrando mi barco, acarretando[8] mi armario de marinero como el tallismán[9] de mi mala suerte.

A summary of the above non-standard usages appears below with suggested alternates representing standard Mexican usages.

First Composition: (10 non-standard usages) 1. para, 2. sobre, 3. con, 4. add, 5. parecidas, 6. las, 7. contribuciones, 8. tenían, 9. Add, 10. Omit.

Second Composition: (8 non-standard usages) 1. pensaba, 2. ningún, 3. concepto, 4. aquí, 5. pensamientos, 6. 6. conceptos, 7. México, 8. pensamientos.

Fifth Composition: (5 non-standard usages): 1. senas, 2. Omit, 3. asistir, 4. Omit, 5. con.

Ninth Composition: (9 non-standard usages): 1. paráiso, 2. qué, 3. Omit, 4. parar, 5. Omit, 6. fortalecía, 7. Omit, 8. cargando, 9. talisman.

As can be seen from the above examples, the teaching of writing to Chicanos at an advanced level comparable to third or fourth year college Spanish, involves an understanding of standard Spanish, regional Spanish, English interference and anomolous usages. Our goal as stated at the outset is to develop skills in standard Mexican Spanish as an additional dialect so that the student can become biloqual. We should note, however, that we are not dealing with a simple division between a regional dialect and a standard dialect with a monolingual Spanish speaking country. The Chicano student is bilingual to a greater or lesser extent and demonstrates characteristics that go beyond those of a regional dialect spoken in Mexico or in other parts of the Spanish speaking world. Typically, he comes from a bilingual region and his schooling has been in English. Thus, careful attention must be paid to the developing of exercises and materials which will lead to biloquialism.

BIBLIOGRAPHY

Anderson, Theodore. 1974. "The Role of the Teacher in a Bilingual Community." Hispania 57: 927-932.

Floyd, Mary Elizabeth. 1976. "Verb Usage and Language Variety in Colorado Spanish." Unpublished Doctoral disser-
sertation, University of Colorado.

Garcia, Nasario. 1976. "To Learn or Not to Learn Standard
Spanish--That is Not the Question," in Valdés Fallis and
Rodolfo Garcia (1976a), pp. 29-37.

Lozano, Anthony. G. 1964. "A Study of Spoken Styles in Colombian Spanish." Unpublished Doctoral dissertation,
University of Texas, Austin.

Ross, L. Ronald. 1975. "La lengua castellana en San Luis,
Colorado." Unpublished Doctoral dissertation, University
of Colorado.

Teschner, Richard V., Garland Bills, and Jerry R. Craddock,
Ed. 1975. Spanish and English of United States Hispan-
os: A Critical, Annotated, Linguistic Bibliography.
Arlington, Virginian: Center for Applied Linguistics.

Valdés Fallis, Guadalupe and Rodolfo García-Moya, Eds. 1976a.
Teaching Spanish to the Spanish Speaking: Theory and
Practice. San Antonio, Texas.

Valdés Fallis, Guadalupe. 1976b. "Pedagogical Implications
of Teaching Spanish to the Spanish speaking in the
United States." In Valdés Fallis and Rodolfo Garcia-
Moya. pp. 3-27.

CHAPTER 7

Language Switching in Chicano Spanish
Linguistic Norm Awareness

Florence Barkin
Arizon State University

The fact that English has influenced Chicano Spanish is
not all surprising. We are indeed amazed that a conquered
people since the military defeat of Mexico by the United
States have been able to withstand the constant linguistic
pressure from the Anglo-American majority who pride themselves on pursuing an English-only policy.

The present investigation addresses itself to the
curious phenomenon of language (commonly called code-
switching)[1] in the speech of Chicano migrant workers in
Florida.[2] According to Christian and Christian (1966:291),
the migrant Spanish speaker exemplifies an intensification of
the economic and social problems experienced by other Spanish
speakers in the United States:

> Generally the least acculturated and the
> least educated of all the Spanish
> speakers in the Southwest, they have been
> imprisoned in this position generation by
> the circumstances of their work. They
> have developed a migratory subculture.

Although 1970 Census Bureau statistics indicate a very small
number of persons of Mexican origin in Florida, these figures
are deceptive due to the difficulty in accumulating accurate
data on such mobile people.[3] There are not statistics specifically geared to the migrant population. Therefore, when
the survey is taken in Florida, many residents are not considered permanent while others, temporarily in other other
states, are left out of the analysis. Unlike many other
areas to which Chicanos migrate, Flordia is beginning to
become their permanent residence particularly due to the long
growing season and promise of work 8 to 10 months a year.
Unfortunately, a truly reliable census would be very difficult. Interestingly enough, none of the Chicanos inter-

102

viewed during this investigation has ever been approached by a census taker!

In pursuit of our goal of studying Chicano bilingualism, we sought information from three principal sources: 1) A revised version of Wolck's Sociolinguistic background questionnaire (1969). 2) Pictorial questionnaires such as Sapon's Pictorial Linguistic Interview Manual (PLIM) (1957) and pictures taken from newpapers, magazines and the Sear's catalogue. 3) Relaxed conversational situations between bilinguals, taped by residents of the migrant camps. We analyzed our linguistic data according to Haugen's three categories of loanwords (1953): unassimilated, partly assimilated and wholly assimilated. The present paper is concerned with unassimilated loanwords, phonologically English, but used in our 33 informants Spanish.[4]

In this investigation we hoped to elicit "casual" speech, that is, the type of speech in which ordinary conversations are held and ordinary conversations are held and ordinary details of living discussed.

However, we had to be constantly aware of the informants' speech changing at any time from casual to formal. Bloomfield (1933:497) states the problem well:

> ... the observer who sets out to study a strange language or a local dialect, often gets data from his informants, only to find them using entirely different forms when they speak among themselves. They count these latter forms inferior, and are ashamed to give them to the observer. An observer may thus record a language entirely unrelated to the one he is looking for.

In order to avoid formal discourse, in which informants attempt to polish their speech when dealing with an outside interview, Labov (1972) suggests three instances in which casual and relaxed speech often occur: prior to the interview, during interruptions by outsiders, and following an interviews. While every effort was made to gain as much information as possible during the interviews, in the present study, much of the observation and recording took place before and after.

Interestingly enough, from the frequency of unadapted English borrowings in our informants' speech, we are able to gain insight into their command of Spanish. We have isolated certain variables to determine why some speakers (No. 2, 3, 5, 6, 10, 11, 17, 21, and 31) have incorporated so many unadapted English form into their Spanish, when identifying drawings in our pictorial questionnaire while others (Nos. 1, 4, 7-9, 14, 16, 18, and 21-30) have utilized so few.

Of the nine informants whose interviews each yielded more than 20 unaltered English loanwords, eight were born in Texas and one in Flordia. None was from Mexico. Moreover, except for informants 3's mother, the informants' parents were _also_ born in this country, making the informants themselves all second generation Americans at the very least. In addition, each of the above informants has been a migrant for several years. With the exception of Informant 17, each has attended monolingual English rather than Spanish-English bilingual schools. According to their interviews, most of these migrants are more proficient in English on a formal, academic level, though they hardly use English in migrant camps where most of the inhabitants are bilingual and prefer speaking Spanish with their family and friends. Consequently, even though their Spanish is inadequate, they use it as their primary means of communication, relying upon English lexical items for frequent assistance. Thus, due to their vocabulary deficiencies in Spanich, these informants borrowed directly from English when identifying objects in the pictorial questionnaire. We attribute their extensive use of unadapted English words to the following: 1. The questionnaire itself represented an academic exercise calling upon their formal education and thus their knowledge of English: 2. Lack of Knowledge of the Spanish equivalent; 3. Greater convenience of an English item (the first word entering the speaker's mind); 4. Speaker's inability to recognize the boundaries between English and Spanish, i.e. lack of awareness of linguistics norms.

Each of the above factors (or a combination of them) called for the use of English words, within a Spanish utterance, in isolation or in chains. English in their Spanish, rather than carrying rhetorical significance, represented an auxiliary tool helping the informants complete the interview in Spanish (or in what they considered to be Spanish).

However, the vast majority of our informants did not rely on direct English borrowings. If they borrow any lexical items at all, they tended to assimilate them into their Spanish. We have divided these latter informants into three main categories: 1. Mexican emigrants who already spoke Spanish before they learned English (Nos. 18, 21, 24, 25, 29); 2. Bilinguals born in the U.S., some of whom had recently decided to settle in Florida and had participated in bilingual programs either there or in Texas (Nos. 1, 7, 8, 14, 16, 27); 3. Other Bilinguals. Some had studied Spanish as a second language in high school. (Nos. 4, 9, 22, 23, 26, 28, 30).

All speakers included in the above categories had two things in common: 1. They were aware of the linguistic norms of at least one of the two languages, and, 2. They were sensitive to the separate identity of Spanish and English. Consequently, if they used elements of one while speaking, they prefaced their switch by either hesitating, explaining the reasons for it, or by saying something like, "or as you say in English."

The informants in the first category each used fewer than four unassimilated English loans in their Spanish. Since they were born in Mexico, they spoke speaking schools. Their heritage was Mexican rather than the dual Mexican-American cultural heritage of some of our other informants. Because of their proficiency in Spanish, and their awareness of the Spanish norm, they did not need English either to fill in gaps in their Spanish or to express affective connotations to their peers.

Bilinguals in the second category were born in the U.S. Since many decided to settle in Florida, they needed English to function in a primarily American community. The fact that they had participated in bilingual programs in school made them extremely sensitive to the norms of both languages. Although they were able to speak either language without demonstrating any influence from the other, when speaking to each other they switched back and forth from Spanish to English. This language-switching was used to communicate certain

certain affective connotations and confidentiality when speaking to those of similar cultural background. Although they frequently switched between Spanish and English in informal situation with their peers, they seldom relied upon English to fill in gaps in their Spanish. Rather than use an English word during their Spanish interview, they preferred to skip on to the next drawing. Informant 1 is a good example of a bilingual in this category. She showed no evidences of English in her Spanish and vice versa. However, when in the company of her Chicano friends and with her siblings, she frequently switched back and forth between Spanish and English. Interestingly enough, when speaking to her own mother, she always spoke Spanish even though her mother knew some English. Informant 1 was extremely sensitive to her use of both languages within the same utterance. If a monolingual in either language, or someone unfamiliar to her entered the room while she was using both languages interchangeably, she would automatically revert to fluent use of either of the two languages. Although these shifts do not cause changes in the understanding of the conversational content, they resulted in a more or less natural "feeling." These shifts were not merely mechanical as were the shifts talked about in the above section. Rather they were a rhetorical device carrying meaning.

Alternating between languages often creates a valuable atmosphere for sensitive communications. Ornstein (1972:83) notes that bilinguals often function more adequately than "an outsider who manipulates the two languages in a 'linear' fashion."

Denison (1971) interpets switching as a skill developed because of sociolingustic norms of expectation. He claims that participants are able to create social situations by skillful switching of varieties of language within a community. His observation can be extended to include bilingual switching between two languages as well as monolingual between the dialects of the same language.

Diebold (1965:141) observed that "a bilingual under emotional stress may revert to the language spoken when comparable emotions have been experienced in the past." Gumperz and Hernandez-Ch. (1971) have also found similar results in their study of classroom interaction among Mexican

Americans. They observe that ideas and experiences are typically Mexican-American while English serves to introduce most new information. Sometimes Spanish is used to amplify the speaker's intent. Mackey (1966) has expressed the need for more research in the field of emotional stress and its relationship to bilingual switching. Evidently, he, too, has observed certain correlations which have aroused his curiosity.

Joshua Fishman contends that interlocutors may vary in the extent to which they switch languages depending on their role-relationships to each other. For example, if an individual speaking to his boss interprets the relationship as a strictly formal one, he is less likely to switch than if the boss were his close friend. In the case of Florida informants, particular concern was taken with the character of the role-relationship being developed. The more informal and casual the role relationship, the more often we found language switching. In the same vein, Ferguson (1964) observes that in many languages there is a style specific to the situation of an adult addressing an infant. Brown and Gilman's study of "tu" and "vous" (1960) shows that the selection is based upon the relationship between the sender and receiver. As Ervin-Tripp (1968) indicates, a shift from one language to another among bilinguals can mark the same contrasts as a sociolinguistic variation in monolinguals. Thus, the interlocutor's perception of each other's roles often determines their speech choices.

Switching may be either conscious or unconscious. It often produces an intentionally humorous effect, as Haugen (1953) so aptly points out. He reports that his American Norwegian informants often make use of ortholgraphic or phonetic similarities between Norwegian and English words to create a humorous result. At other times, the tone of the message alone may determine when and where a switch will occur. Blom and Gumperz (1971) have observed that even when speakers can recognize the social meaning of switching, they may not be able to control it consciously when engaged in bilingual conversations. The role-relationships are predetermined and the necessity to switch is inherent. The very nature of the relationship between the interlocutors and the topic under discussion prevent the speaker from controlling his language alternations.

Even though the individual may not be able to control his switching under certain circumstances, we know that the phenomenon of switching itself is never random. It follows certain co-occurrence rules which determine whether a switch can take place in a certain position or at a specified time in a conversation. Co-currence rules underline the existence of norms for switching. Therefore metaphorical switching is possible for the purpose of establishing new meanings and insights. Fishman (1972:43) states that:

> Metaphorical switching is a luxury that can be afforded only by those that comfortably share not only the same set of situational norms but also the same view as to their inviolability.

Since most of us are members of several speech communities, switching could be misunderstood if used within a community unaware of its impact. However, Ervin-Tripp (1964) points out that norms of correctness are generated by the members of the stable bilingual communities which largely interact with other bilinguals. According to Pandit (1969:255)[5] "whether it is stylistic variation among the varieties of one language or whether it is language switching across mutually unintelligible varieties, variation is rule-governed behavior."

Gumperz (1966) realized than any encounter between speakers always conveys more than the cognitive content of the message. Although on the surface the choice appears random, people whose speech demonstrates a great deal of interference may be very sensitive in conveying social meanings by language switching. (Gumperz, 1971). As Dell Hymes (1967:9) relates:

> No normal person and no normal community is limited in repertoire to a single variety of code to an unchanging monotony which would preclude the possibility of indicating respect, insolence, mock-seriousness, humor, role-distance, etc. by switching from one code variety to another.

Switching is more than a merely mechanical process of language alternation. It is a rhetorical device which carries meaning. Kimple, Cooper, and Fishman (1969:134) note that the shifts in the use of the two languages may not cause changes in the comprehension of the conversation's content. However, they contend that the switches may result in the feeling that the conversation has become more or less "natural."

The following material has been extracted from a number of taped, unrehearsed conversations by Chicano informants. These informants were not aware of the presence of the tape recorder. Therefore, we can assume that these conversations are representative of their everyday interactions with each other. Each conversation included in the text is followed by a detailed analysis of its sociolinguistic content.

Content 1:

Jorge: Hey, Luis, when you gonna play baseball?

Luis: No sé cuando.

Jorge: Cúando vas a ir?

Luis: Mañana

Jorge: I wanna go.

Luis: What you gonna do. Qué vas a hacer, hey?

The topic is baseball, a familiar American sport. Jorge proceeds to ask about it in English since his experiences with the game have been either in school or on television, on the radio or in the newspapers. However, Luis, in interpreting the boys' familiar role-relationship, answers in Spanish. He often used either Spanish, English, or a combination of the two when speaking with Jorge or many of his peers. In response to Luis's Spanish statement, Jorge continues in Spanish. Here we see a continuation of the language immediately preceding as well as a change in topic, i.e. Luis's forthcoming vacation. Luis continues in Spanish. Thus far, Luis has not uttered a word in English. Jorge reverts to the language he began speaking, i.e. English.

109

Here Luis responds with his first words in English, "What you gonna do?" However, he returns to Spanish, repeating his English question, "Qué vas a hacer?" He concludes his comments in English in with the interjection, "hey?" Here Luis expresses the close role-relationship with Jorge. Naturally, the use of the Spanish translation adds to the emphasis of the English, "What you gonna do?" The following chart is a schematic representation of the conversation, noting the reasons for each language's use.

Speaker	Language	Reason
Jorge	English	Topic
Luis	Spanish	Role-Relationship
Jorge	Spanish	Preceding Language Role-Relationship
Luis	Spanish	Preceding Lanugage Role-Relationship
Jorge	English	Initiating Lanugage
Luis	English Spanish English	Preceding Lanugage Emphasis Role-Relationship

From this example, we can extract various causes for language switching. First, the creation of a certain social situation, which becomes clear through the choice of topic and the close relationship between the two boys. The relaxing atmosphere of the close peer relationships opens the conversation up to three possible language choices: The mixture of the two, in the last comment by Luis, can be considered metaphorical since it establishes a new feeling and conveys a new social meaning beyond the words themselves. We perceive mild sarcasm at the unfortunate situation that Jorge will be unable to accompany Luis tomorrow. Here the tone of the message along determines when the switch will occur. Thus the rhetorical device of switching does not cause a change in the conversation's content, but rather conveys a new connotation. Here it is one of sarcasm because of the inability to change an already planned event.

110

Conversation 2:

Daughter 1: Have you put out everything of everything?
Mother: Sí, y más.

Daughter 1: Look at those... they look del... Everything is delicious.

Daughter 2: A mí no me gusta. Tiene a funny taste to it. It's got a taste como...

The family is at a picnic. Everyone is seated at the table. The first daughter initiates the conversation in English. The mother responds in Spanish. Although she speaks little English, she evidently understands it perfectly. Daughter 1 continues in English almost as if there has been no lanugage switch by her mother. Interestingly enough, Daughter 2 interjects a contradictory comment in Spanish, interrupting herself in English and switching again to Spanish. Let us examine the following chart.

Speaker	Language	Reason
Daughter 1	English	Not clear from context
Mother	Spanish	Natural language in family interaction
Daughter 1	English	Initiating Language
Daughter 2	Spanish	Contradiction
	English	English idiom
	Spanish	Continuation of first thought.

In conversation 2, Daughter 1 spoke English without any switching. her mother also maintained all communication in Spanish. However, Daughter 2 finds herself caught in between communicating with her mother in Spanish and with her sister in English or a mixture of the two. Daughter 2 demonstrates a carefuly role variation in language choice: Mother: Spanish, Sister: English, or Spanish and English. Daughter 2 also shifts abruptly from her sister's comment, therefore setting her statement off "from the more gradual transition

111

between styles in monolingual repertoires." (Gumperz, 1971:45).

Conversation 3:

In the following monologue, a woman, Informant 1, is speaking with three of her friends at the Day Care Center. She is relating her friend's trip to Mexico. He hated it. Se acabo el agua and sometimes they'd be taking a bath and se acaba el agua. In some hotels tiene que flush the toilets enchandole agua. So dice que he had a terrible time, ya know.

This informant spoke fluent English and Spanish. However, she admitted to speaking a mixture of two when speaking with her friends. She knows they understand her and she feels closer to them when switching from one language to the other. As we can see, the informant alternates 11 times between the two languages. In the second sentence the informant switches twice. Each switch is separated by the conjunction and. However, in the third sentence, one clause includes both Spanish and Enlgish. Flush the toilets appears in English as part of the Spanish clause beginning with tiene que. In this isolated instance, the speaker seems to have forgotten the equivalent expression in Spanish, therefore substituting the English version. Here the informant clearly indicates the casual switching process alternately using both Spanish and English. Let us examine the following chart.

Speaker	Language	Sections
Informant 1	English	He hated it.
	Spanish	Se acabó el agua.
	English	and sometimes they'd be taking a bath.
	Spanish	se acaba el agua.
	English	In some hotels
	Spanish	tiene que
	English	flush the toilets

112

Spanish	echandole agua
English	So
Spanish	Dice que
English	He had a terrible time, ya know.

Here we see a total of four sentences. Only the first appears totally in English. In one sentence, "In some hotels, tiene que flush the toilets echandole agua" we observe three switches. According to Gumperz and Hernandez-Ch. (1971:317) this type of language mixture is not rate. "It is very persistent wherever minority language groups come in close contact with majority language groups under conditions of rapid social change." In the above monologue, not all instances of Spanish words in the text are necessarily examples of language switching. They are fixed expressions such as dice que that are normally part of the bilingual's style while speaking English. Gumperz and Hernandez-Ch. (1971:318) compare these to Yiddish expressions like nebish, oi gewalt characteristic of in-group English style of some American Jews. They function as stylistic ethnic identity markets. Gumperz and Hernandez-Ch. (1971:1) cite the following example:

Woman: Well, I'm glad that I met you. O.K.?

M.: Andales, pues. (O.K. SWELL) And do come again, mmm?

"The andale pues is given in response to the woman's O.K., as if to say: 'although we are strangers we have the same background and should get to know each other better.'" In our text, the only fixed ethnic identity marker in Spanish is dice que. However, in English we observe English interjections i.e. So, ya know. Gumperz and Hernandez-Ch. (1971) also note some examples of true language switching consisting of entire sentences inserted into other language text and some examples of change within single sentences. As in their examples, our text includes syntactic connections enabling both parts to be viewed as independent sentences.

113

Se acabó el agua.   And sometimes they'd be taking a
bath. (and)

Se acaba el agua.

Se acabo el agua.   And sometimes they'd be taking a
bath. (and)

Se acaba el agua.

In our text, concrete ideas and expressions relating to the
Mexican-American surroundings are stated in English:

"and sometimes they'd be taking a bath and..."

"In some hotels..."

"flush the toilets..."

Gumperz and Hernández-Ch. (1971:335) observe that "psychological" terminology or expressions such as "pacify",
"relax," "I am a biter," are rarely used in typically
Mexican-American settings. Informant 1 appears to follow
this pattern, using English in the following cases:

"He hated it."

"He had a terrible time..."

Through our study of casual conversation among this
group of informants, we find that language switching is a
common stylistic device. Its initiation is often determined
by the topic, place and role-relationship of the interlocutors. It is often adds subltle information to the conversation although it does not alter the message. Certain
expressions in each language are fixed and occur within the
context of the other. Since some of our informants rely
heavily on switching, they appear extremely sensitive to the
relationship between language and text.

The third group of informants did not switch languages
but were also extremely conscious of linguistic norms.
Informant 9, who never went to bilingual school, learned
Spanish as a primary language at home, and as a second

language in school. He restricted his use of Spanish strictly to his immediate family. Due to his attempt to avoid being classified as a Chicano, to his impending marriage to a monolingual "Anglo," and to his awareness that the interview was to take place in Spanish, he did not switch into English either to express affective connotations or to fill in the words he did not know in Spanish. Since his Spanish was inadequate, he was unable to identify many PLIM drawings. However, rather than use English equiavalents, he skipped all drawings whose Spanish equivalents he did not know. On the other hand, since his English was quite fluent, he did not need to rely upon Spanish, expecially since his largely American contacts would not understand his Spanish or his alternation between the two languages. Even if his Spanish were proficient enough to allow for the type of switching, which adds new connotations to an utterance, the social stigma attached to this mixture would be even greater than that attached to Spanish in his "Anglo" environment. That is to say that on first glance an American would assume that switching was a sign of inability to express himself in either language.

Those informants (category 1) who laced their Spanish with unadapted English words during the pictorial interview appeared to be floundering along the border between the two lexicons in an effort to fill out their inadequate Spanish vocabulary with English words needed in order to function in Spanish within the bilingual community. These speakers, all born in the United States, have seldom, if ever, been exposed to monolingual Spanish speakers. We speculate that in this situation they will continue to use English terms unconsciously.

The only group of informants who switched back and forth from Spanish to English as an expression of intimacy and ethnic solidarity was the second, all at least second generation Americans, and sensitively aware of the question of norms. They were proficient in both languages and could communicate in either one or a mixture of the two in certain situations. We believe that language switching among these Chicanos has for them a certain emotional and cultural significance. It connotes an ethnic solidarity, a recognition of a shared dual heritage. They are, in a sense, proclaiming their easy familiarity with both cultures. This alternation is more than a superficial hodgepodge of the two languages: it in fact symbolized their identification with a close-know group with a people and a cause in a society so alien, as if to say:

> Listen, listen, I am American. I speak
> English. But I am one of you, a Chicano,
> of beautiful heritage. You are my
> brother. We are of one and the same;
> part American, part Mexican, los dos.[6]

Educators should recognize the differences between Chicanos who switch from Spanish to English they cannot distinguish the two languages, or from an inability to recall Spanish lexical items, and those who use languages switching deliberately in order to convey additional affective meaning. In the case of Chicanos who are able to express themselves well in either language but consciously choose to switch between Spanish and English while talking with each other, we should recognize this habit of what it is, namely an assertion of their dual cultural heritage.

Rather than criticize bilingual youngsters for switching back and forth between two languages, once it is determined and why they switch, educators can develop programs specifically geared to their individual linguistic needs.

NOTES

[1]Although "code-switching" has come to refer to alternation between two languages and between dialects of the same language, this author considers code the result of the switching process, (the utterances in which both languages or dialects are found), since that result implies many of the in-group connotations of a code. Thus, the present study will refer to language switching and language alternation rather than code-switching.

[2]The principal migrant worker camps are found near Orlando, around Apopka and Ocoee, near Miami and West Palm Beach and on the West Coast in the Homestead area.

[3]1970 United States Department of Census Bureau Statistics list 9,072,602 persons of Spanish origin in the United States of whom 4,532, 435 are of Mexican origin. Only 20,869 persons of Mexican origin are from Florida.

[4]See Informant Background Chart.

[5]Commentary following Gumperz (1971): How can we describe and measure the behavior of bilingual groups?

[6]I have taken the liberty to create this passage in order to represent the feelings of ethnic identity expressed to me by Chicano informants, particularly those acutely aware of linguistic norms.

INFORMATION BACKGROUND CHART

Informants	Sex	Age	Origin	Occu-pation	Spouse's Origin	Spouse's Occupation	Mother's Origion	Father's Origin
1	F	18	Virginia	Day Care Counselor	-	-	Texas	Texas
2	F	25	Texas	Laborer	Texas	Laborer	Texas	Texas
3	M	17	Texas	Laborer	Mexico	Laborer	Texas	Mexico
4	F	25	Texas	Housewife	Mexico	Laborer	Arizona	California
5	F	19	Texas	Housewife	Texas	Laborer	Texas	Texas
6	F	43	Texas	Laborer	Mexico	Laborer	Texas	Texas
7	F	13	Florida	Student	-	-	Mexico	Mexico
8	F	11	Florida	Student	-	-	Mexico	Mexico
9	M	19	Texas	Gen. Elec. Employee	-	-	Mexico	Mexico
10	F	16	Texas	Nurseryman	Mexico	Nursery-man	Texas	Texas
11	F	32	Texas	Housewife	Texas	Laborer	Texas	Texas
12	F	12	Texas	Student	-	-	Mexico	Mexico
13	F	21	Texas	Student	-	-	Texas	Mexico
14	M	18	Texas	Laborer	Texas	Laborer	Texas	Mexico
15	F	24	Miss.	Housewife	Alabama	Steel Worker	Mexico	Mexico

118

Informants	Sex	Age	Origin	Occu-pation	Spouse's Origin	Spouse's Occupation	Mother's Origion	Father's Origin
16	F	22	Texas	Housewife	Texas	Laborer	Mexico	Texas
17	F	14	Florida	Student	-	-		
18	F	46	Mexico	Housewife	Mexico	Laborer	Texas	Texas
19	F	18	Texas	Student	-	-	Mexico	Mexico
20	F	25	Texas	Housewife	Texas	Laborer	Texas	Texas
21	F	29	Texas	Laborer/ Housewife	Texas	Laborer	Texas	Texas
22	F	23	Mexico	Housewife	Texas	Laborer	Mexico	Mexico
23	F	31	Texas	Housewife	Texas	Laborer	Texas	Mexico
24	M	19	Texas	Laborer/ Nurseryman	-	-	Texas	Texas
25	M	20	Mexico	Nurseryman	Texas	Nursery-man	Mexico	Mexico
26	F	23	Mexico	Nurseryman	Mexico	Laborer	Mexico	Texas
27	M	20	Texas	Laborer	-	-	Texas	Texas
28	F	5	Texas	Student	-	-	Texas	Texas
29	F	24	Texas	Housewife	Texas	Laborer	Mexico	Mexico
30	F	22	Texas	Housewife	Texas	Laborer	Mexico	Mexico
31	M	12	Texas	Student	-	-	Texas	Texas
32	F	7	Texas	Student	-	-	Texas	Texas
33	M&F	3-7	Texas	Student	-	-	-	-

119

REFERENCES

Blom, Jan-Petier and John J. Gumperz, 1972. Social meaning in lingusitic structure: Code-switching in Norway, in Directions in Sociolinguistics. Ed. by John J. Gumperz and Dell Hymes. Holt, Rinehart and Winston, Inc. 407-434.

Bloomfield, Leonard, 1933. Language. New York. Henry Holt and Company.

Christian, Chester C., Jr. and Jane MacNab Christian. 1966. Spanish language and culture in the Southwest. Language loyalty in the United States. Ed. by Joshua Fishman. The Hague. London. Paris. Mouton and Co.

Denison, N. 1969. Sociolingusitics and pluralingualism. Actes duXe Congres International des linguistes 1. Bucharest. 551-559.

Diebold, A. Richard R. 1965. A survey of psycholinguistic research, 1954-1964. Psycholinguistics: A survey of of theory and research problems. Ed. by Charles E. Osgood and Thomas A. Sebeok. Bloomington, Indiana University Press.

Ervin-Tripp, Susan, 1964. Language and TAT content in bilinguals. Language acquisition and communicative choice. Stanford University Press, 1973. 45-61. Originally published in Journal of Abnormal and Social Psychology 68, 6. 500-57.

  1968. An analysis of the interaction of language, topic and listener. Readings in the Sociology of Lanugage. Ed. by Joshua A. Fishman. The Hague, Paris, London. Mouton and Co. 192-211.

Fishman, Joshua A. 1972. The Sociology of Language: An interdisciplinary Social Science approach to language in society. Rowley, Mass., Newbury House Publishers.

Fishman, Joshua A., Robert L. cooper, and Roxana Ma et al. 1971. Bilingualism in the barrio. Indiana University Language Science Monograph Series, No. 7. Bloomington, Research Center for Language Sciences, Indiana University.

Gumperz, John. 1964. Lingusitic and social interaction in two communities. Language in social groups. Stanford, California. Stanford University Press, 1971. 151-176. Originally published in American Anthropologist 66:6, Part 2, The ethnography of communication, Ed. by J. J. Gumperz and Dell Hymes.

1976a. On the lingustic markers of bilingual communication. The Journal of Social Issues, Vol. XXIIJ, No. 48-57.

1976b. The relation of linguistic to social categories. Language in social groups, Stanford, California. Stanford University Press, 1971. 220-229. Originally published in a Field Manual for cross-cultural study of the acquisition of communicative competence. Ed. by D.I. Slobin. Berkely, University of California, 84-92.

1970. Verbal strategies in multilingual communication. Monograph Series on Language and Linguistics. No. 23, Ed. by James E. Alatis. Washington, D. C. Georgetown University Press. 129-148.

1971. in collaboration with Eduardo Hernandez-Ch. Bilingualism bidialectalism, and classroom interaction. Language in Social Groups. Stanford University Press, 310-339. Ed. by courtney B. Cazden, V. P. John, and D. Hymes. New York, Teachers College Press.

Haugen, Einar. 1953. The Norwegian Language in America. A study in bilingual behavior. Philadelphia, University of Pennsylvania Press, (reprinted 1969) Indiana University Press.

Hymes, Dell. 1967. Models of the interaction of language and social setting. The Journal of Social Issues. Vol. XXLII No. 2, 8-28.

Kimple, James, Jr. and Robert L. Cooper and Joshua A. Fishman. 1969. Language switching and the interpretation of conversations. Lingua 23. 127-134.

Labov, William. 1966. The social stratification of English in New York City. Washington, D.C. Center for Applied Linguistics.

Mackey, William. 1966. The measurement of bilingual behavior. The Canadian Psychologist, Vol. 7a, No. 2. 75-91.

1970. Interference, integration and the synchronic fallacy. Monograph Series on languages and linguistics, No. 23. James E. Atalis. Georgetown University Press. 195-227.

Ornstein, Jacob. 1972. Toward a classification of Southwest Spanish nonstandard variants. Linguistics, 94. 70-87.

Sapon, Stanley M. 1957. A pictorial lingustic interview manual.

Wölck, Wolfgang. 1969. An attitude test devised for 'El Proyecto BQC'. See El Proyecto BQC: Metogologia de una encuesta sociolinguistica sobre el bilingualismo Quechua-Castellano. In: Lingüística e indigenismo moderno de America. Ed. by G. J. Parker, A. G. Lozano, and R. Ravines.

CHAPTER 8

ORDER VERSUS CONFLICT SOCIETIES:

THE DILEMMA OF BICULTURAL EDUCATION

Geraldo Kaprosy (University of Texas at El Paso)
Robert St. Clair (University of Louisville)

INTRODUCTION

Metaphors provide a way of seeing something. They create perspectives for social behavior and also lend some insight into theoretical models which underly scientific research (Brown, 1978:78-79). They also generate attitudes toward social behavior by defining the context of a situation or by providing a plan of social expectation. Therefore, the study of metaphor as a model of social behavior can be informative.

In the field of bilingual and bicultural education, there are two dominant metaphors which are best characterized as order and conflict models of society (Horton, 1966). These models make different assumptions about social interaction and generate different expectations for resolving issues that occur within the public domain. Their disparities are best characterized, however, in their definition and treatment of social problems and -in particular -their approaches to the problem of bicultural dissonance.

In the order model of society, social problems are defined in terms of maintaining the system or the status quo. When differences occur, they are said to threaten the norm (Becker, 1973). They are considered to be deficiencies within the system as thereby constitute a form of deviance (Szasz, 1970) which, it is feared, can lead to the social disorganization of the system or anomie. To regain structural integrity in an order society, homeostasis or a balancing mechanism is required and this is accomplished only when the health of the system is restored. If the system is to remain in working order, it is argued, there must be conformity and adherence to the norm. To save the system from impending disaster within the framework of a law and order society, social problems are sometimes resolved by radical means. In the most severe cases of threatened disorder, for example, social surgery is openly advocated. The usual strategy for restoring the system into balance, however, is through adherence to the norm. This is sometimes referred to in the literature as mainstreaming or the ideology of accomodation. The metaphor of the order society, then, is one of mental illness. When social problems occur, they are seen as forms of illness which must be contained by segregation or social surgery. Within the order society of the United States during the turn of the century, the metaphor of social illness dictated that reservations be set up and ghettos or barrios be created to contain those who were not welcomed by the system. In the case of Germany during the Third Reich, on the other hand, the final solution was one of radical surgery from the body politic.

The conflict model of society differs substantially from its law and order counterpart in the definition and the treatment of social problems. It assumes that when a group obtains power, it attempts to reify its value system and impose its beliefs on others through the process of political socialization. However, this imposition is not a natural one and must be contested and openly negotiated as a form of social reality within the public domain. Consequently, the concept of alienation or interpersonal estrangement (Schacht, 1970: 11) is inherent within the framework of a conflict society. In order to understand change and the conflict of values that it engenders, one is required to seek solutions in social history, situation ethics, and the negotiation of social reality. Stanford Lyman and Marvin Scott (1970) have developed a model of existential sociology which illustrates the workings of a conflict society. They first raise the question of how is social order possible and note that contrary to political moralists and other advocates of the order society model that social order is the product of human construction. The world is essentially without meaning in that all systems of belief are arbitrary. People must create social order from existential chaos. They must carve out meanings in a world that is meaningless. They must see peace and tranquility in a world in which alienation and insecurity are the fundamental conditions of life. Existence, then, is

a life-long process of becoming. It requires that one view
social action in terms of episodes, encounters and situations. Therefore, the fundamental structure of human action
is conflict. One is constantly in conflict with society.
One is forever fighting the forces of nature; and, one is in
an eternal struggle with one's inner concepts of self.
Social life is one of conflict. It is interesting to note
that Lyman and Scott (1970: 13) cite Niccolo Macchiavelli as
their protagonist in the drama of social interaction. He saw
public life in terms of deceptions, lies, and broken
promises. Those who cannot cope with the world of multiple
realities, he notes, are made to believe in illusions. Life
for Macchiavelli is a game in which meanings must be created
and mediated through language. It is language, Lyman and
Scott (1970:18) note, that allows one to symbolize and communicate one's desires, feelings, and thoughts and to
negotiate these emotions and believes within the public
domains of social reality. What is significant about the
conflict model of society is that it treats social problems
as mere differences in belief. Those with power have the
ability to create and define social problems. They have
within their institutions the mechanisms for controlling
social behavior and channeling social expectations. However,
their positions within the power structure are not absolute.
This is because power is a reciprocal concept (Jacobsen,
1972) and those who exercise it do so in proportion to those
who counter it within the political arena. This has become
particularly evident recently when the power elite (Mills,
1956) has been challenged by those who have advocated
minority rights (Greenbaum, 1974).

The distinction between order and conflict societies is
a significant one. Both models present illustrative
metaphors (Brown, 1977: 78) of how minorities are viewed
within the context of bilingual and bicultural education.
For those who adhere to the law and order framework, for
example, minorities are seen as a threat to the homogeneity
of the system. Consequently, they become objects for mainstreaming legislation, or segregation policies. They have
been defined as the social problem. But, within the context
of a conflict society, minorities are seen as just another
group in a system where heterogeneity is the expected form of
ecological balance. Social reality is not defined in
ultimate terms by one group for all (Parenti, 1974). Differences are not interpreted as deficits. For the teacher

in minority education, these distinctions are important as they provide insight into the foundations of their educational structures.

THE TEACHER AS SOCIAL ENFORCER

Language education is a socio-political process. But, school teachers are generally unaware of this. They have been taught that their tasks revolve around methodolgoy. When taking courses in the language arts, their concerns are with the assessment of reading skills, the testing of language proficiency, the measurement of reading comprehension, the acquisition of lexical forms, the analysis of lingusitic forms, techniques of expository writing, etc. In each case the focus is on method. The basic question is: How? Even when content is the concern it is downgraded and the issue becomes one of how to teach content. Within a conflict society model, this view of the educator is to be expected. The teacher is the social enforcer for the system. He or she regulates the flow of minorities into the mainstream. But, in an order society model, the teacher is not only a social enforcer, but also an agent of change. Therefore, the crucial question is not how something is done, but also why it is being done. Who benefits? What values are being taught in the hidden curriculum? How are minorities portrayed in the literature? Are they seen as heroes or villains? Are they treated as insiders or outsiders? Obviously, language education does involve much more than mere questions of methodology. This aspect of political socialization is seen most clearly in institutional labelling.

Howard Becker (1973) argues that pejorative labels which are mediated through language are the result of the socio-political process. He challenges the "bad seed" model of deviancy which has characterized psychological research. He expresses sincere doubts about the Freudian model which views deviancy in terms of mental illness and in this sense he shares the concerns of Thomas Szasz (1970) and other (Brown, 1973; Scheff, 1977) who find this to be the wrong metaphor for defining and treating those who differ from the mainstream of social acceptibility (Kittrie, 1974). Although what Becker has to say about deviancy involves such case studies as the marihuana user, the dance musician, and mental illness, it does have much to say about other political and social minorities within an order society framework. It pertains, for example, to those who have been labelled as mentally retarded, emotionally disturbed. And, it applies to those who are now being called "culturally deprived" or "linguistically deprived."

There are three components involved in the process of labelling. The first requires that someone is threatened. The patterns of social reality which one provided comfort are being attenuated. Under such conditions, the symbols of status have become tainted and the positive memories of the past no longer have value and respect within the larger public domain of social interaction. Under these circumstances, the moral entrepreneur emerges and demands that those who are creating this state of cognitive dissonance (Festinger, 1957) be eliminated from the system. This crusader of political moralism (Lipset and Raab, 1978:12) views the world in absolutist terms and is uncompromising in the political arena. When the moral entrepreneur has the backing of the power elite or when such a person is able to establish a power base through lobbying, the result is usually social legislation. The second component in the process of labelling occurs when the various agencies of government are put into the situation of enforcing the new laws. These public servants may not share the political moralism of the crusader, but they do view their obligations to the system which has provided them with employment. Enforcement, then, becomes merely a task of demonstrating that one is doing a good job at following the letter of the law. But, as Becker (1973:155-156) notes, these social enforcers must prove that they are successful. They must meet a quota. Who are these social enforcers? They turn out to be policemen, teachers, administrators, and other civil servants who depend on federal, state, and private institutions for their income. Finally, there are the victims of the labelling process. They are the ones who have been publically stigmatized and who suffer verbal abuse. These labels eventually dominate the world view of the victim and create a negative self-concept; and, it is this pejorative definition of self that leads to despair and anxiety in the individual. For some, the solution is suicide; for others, it means having a marginal life.

In discussing social enforcement, Becker (1973:20) demonstrates how the process is not only selective, but also favors the power elite and those who adhere to their legitimation of values. The four kinds of deviant behaviors are defined by the parameters of how one is perceived by the public and how one behaves with regard to the rules and the laws of society (St. Clair, 1979).

	Obedient Behavior	Rule-Breaking Behavior
Perceived as Deviant	FALSELY ACCUSED	PURE DEVIANT
Not Perceived as Deviant	CONFORMING	SECRET DEVIANT

The pure deviant is defined by the collective action of the community as one who is truly an outsider. This label, however, is not absolute. At one time in the history of the United States, for example, women who wanted to participate in the political process were viewed as pure deviants. Also, those who were divorced were deemed as pure deviants. But, times have changed. Now, one who is not divorced is more likely to be considered as non-conforming. The person who is not perceived as deviant and whose behavior is within the law conforms to the system. This is the silent majority within a law and order society. The intersting categories, however, turn out to be those of the secret deviant and the falsely accused. The former, it should be mentioned, belongs to the power elite. When this person drinks too much, such action is excused as social drinking. When this individual steps out of the bounds of propriety, these actions are condoned as eccentricities. When such persons create a raucus and engage in self-indulgence, they are called jet-setters and become models of emulation. The falsely accused, however, is not a part of the power elite. Such a person is a member of the lower economic strata of society and usually belongs to an ethnic minority. It is for this group that all of the pejorative labels have been saved. What they do is seen as crime, drunkedness, loitering, disturbing of the peace, and stepping out of place. When the same actions are done by the secret deviants, however, they are called business ventures, social drinking, sight seeing and tourism, civic celebrations, and slumming.

How does the teacher fit into these discussions of labelling theory? Unfortunately, they play a major role in keeping the status quo. They are among the best social enforcers that the system could ask for. Although they may view themselves in non-political terms, they are definitely political agents. The tests that they administer, for example, favor certain groups over others. The content on their courses create heroes of some groups and villains of others. The options that they offer their students have more to do with the training of the urban working class than with education and cognitive growth (Violas, 1978). What they are teaching is political culture.

LANGUAGE AND POLITICAL CULTURE

Language mediates culture. It provides the medium for the values and the beliefs of communities with which one interacts. When it is aligned with power, language has the capacity to modify the conduct of others through the real or threatened use of rewards and punishments. Language, then, allocates values. It socializes. What is significant for the teacher of minority education, however, is the fact that language also provides the medium for the imparting of political culture. It teaches one how to accept certain orientations toward the system (Mueller, 1976).

One of the ways in which attitudes are incorporated into language is by the creation of a political identity. Children learn rather early under the guise of geography that they belong to a nation. They come to learn of its boundaries and see themselves as being part of this politically defined group. For the child who enters the school system as an immigrant or for the child who is aware of his or her ethnic heritage, this attempt to create a symbolic allegiance can lead to bicultural dissonance. They learn to see themselves as citizens of a new nation, but are at loss in assessing the pejorative labels that have been assigned to their former mother country.

The second means by which political culture is developed

129

is through those social activities which inculcate a belief
in the system. By pledging to the flag and by reciting
portions of the formal documents of the government, a child
soon comes to have trust in the system. They learn to dis-
parage other forms of government and by the time that they
become adults, they have already learned to boast about how
they would not trade their system of government for any other
in the world. They have come to learn respect for their
political institutions and have oriented themselves to the
legitimacy of the system.

Political culture also demands that one learns the
rules of the game and that attitudes of consent be encouraged. By learning respect for the rules of the system,
they are provided with a sense of obligation to work within
its very structure. Riots, revolutions, and civic dis-
turbances are not acceptable. They run contrary to the rules
and its inherent structure which favors the status quo. Behavior in the classroom, then, is a prelude to behavior in
public. The student who respects the system and its rules is
a good citizen. The one that does not is seen as emotionally
disturbed and socially incorrigible. Such students, it is
argued, require discipline. It is interesting to note how
thin the line is between a leader and a rebel. The former is
seen as one who enhances the values of the system and knows
how to play the rules of the game. The latter is also a
leader. However, this person does not work within the system
and plays according to rules which are not legitimate.

Political performance is another important aspect of
political culture. One must learn to become involved in the
system of politics, to have knowledge of public events and
official celebrations, and to take an interest in political
affairs. They should consider the rewards of running for
office and the benefits of interacting with the system. In
their study of civic cultures, Gabriel Almond and Sidney
Verba (1963) categorize people in terms of their interaction
in the political culture. First, there are the parochials
who have no idea of how to influence the system or take
advantage of public legislation. Next, there are the
subjects who take advantage of government and its promulga-
tion, but who are unable to cause demands on the system.
Finally, there are the participants in a civic culture who
not only are able to take advantage of the system, but who
are also able to cause demands on it. Almond and Verba

(1963) envision in the United States as a civic culture and see its citizenry as participants in the political process. However, for the minorities who continue to be labelled and disenfranchized, this assessment is not concomitant with their experience. They feel more like parochials when the issues revolve around social mobility and political power and like subjects when they are the targets of the war on poverty.

Once one is aware of the concept of political culture and the intracacies of labelling theory, the distinction between the order and conflict society and its implications for bilingual and bicultural education becomes more apparent. In the order society, the teacher is a social enforcer and must abide by the dictates of the system and its socio-economic needs (Spring, 1976). In the conflict model of society, the teacher of a bicultural classroom becomes a social agent (Ramirez and Castañeda, 1974). The dilemma for the teacher occurs when he or she wants to change the system, but is working in an institution which reflects an order society mentality. Similarly, the dilemma occurs when social change requires the teacher to become a social agent, but he or she refuses and continues to adhere to a philosophy of political moralism. In each case, there are conflicts of values across cultures and the result is one of bicultural dissonance. Such oscillations between open and closed models of society do occur (Klapp, 1978) and as a consequence the teacher cannot forever hide behind the neutrality of methodology and assessment programs. It is for this reason that the foundations of education should be seen as one of the most significant aspects of pre-service training for bilingual and bicultural education teachers.

THE ILLUSION OF CULTURAL PLURALISM IN AN ORDER SOCIETY

The United States is and always has been an order society. Students of political science and social history have known that contrary to the popular view of social studies classes, elites and not masses govern America (Dye and Zeigler, 1972). The key decisions of a political, economic, and social nature are made by a few within the power elite (Mills, 1956) in a system in which the government is for the few (Parenti, 1974). These elites may form a

131

pyramid or may even divide power and give the illusion of a conflict society, but they nevertheless exist and possess control over such resources as power, wealth, education, prestige, status, skills of leadership, information, knowledge of the system and special organizations (Dye and Zeigler, 1972: 5). As a group, they form a consensus and attempt to reify their values and beliefs. In essence, they establish public policy which favors their concerns and interests. Such concerted effort, it should be noted, is not to be confused with a "conspiracy theory" which readily characterize extremist groups (Lipset and Raab, 1978). Such groups suffer from a lack of historical sense and lack an ability to negotiate and compromise within the public arena. In this sense, they are a political. In addition, they tend to view others in terms of personal threats to their belief system (Hofstadter, 19567). Perhaps, the power elite is best characterized not in terms of a conspiracy, but in terms of a community of interests. What distinguishes it from other groups which also share a community of interests, however, is their possession of power which allows them to favor legislation in their direction and to control access resources. They are the real participants in the civic culture that Almond and Verba (1963) describe in their research of political interaction.

The Founding Fathers who wrote the Constitution of the United States and who founded a new nation were the first elites in this order society. They were not only rich and well-born, but they were also well educated and resourceful. They represented the nation's economic and intellelctual elites. They were the possessors of landed estates. They were the large merchants and the importers of foreign goods. They were the financiers; and, they were the moneylanders. What they possessed in the form of real estates and public bonds and securities were highly disproportionate to the populace of small farmers, debtors, tradesmen, frontiersmen, servants, slaves, and outsiders. The 55 men who wrote the Constitution did not reflect the four million Americans that they claimed to represent. They represented their own interests. What made them different from the aristocracy of Europe is that their status was not ascribed by royal lineage, it was achieved and the criterion for their success in the political arena was directly tied to their talent for acquiring property (Dye and Ziegler, 1972: 27).

For the political scientists of constitutional democracy, the founding of the government of the United States was written to insure the power of the elite. The constitution, Parenti (1974) notes, was framed by financially successful planters, merchants, lawyers, bankers, and creditors and many of them were linked socially by family relationship and commercial interests. But, this information is not new. It has been admirably documented by Charles Beard (1913) in his study of the economic basis of the constitution. What Michael Parenti does add, however, is his analysis of the agenda-setting which underlies the constitution and which favors the status quo and their retention of a power base. To prevent unity of the propertyless majority through public sentiment, the populace had to be compartmentalized into geographically insulated political communities. To prevent the majority from achieving direct political force they were also provided with an indirect form of representation. Hence, the Founding Fathers were guided by direct material and class interests and these were fully reflected in the document that they claimed to have written on behalf of the populace. It is, therefore, an elitist document and was more concerned with the securing of property than with personal liberties. As Michael Parenti notes, the staggering of elections was meant to prevent access to the system by popular demand and the intricacies of checks and balances were meant to insure that the opposition to the power elite would remain fragmented and dispersed.

In his discussion of the power elite, C. Wright Mills (1956) describes the transition which has taken place since the founding of the nation. Power is now organized into institutions. These may be at the corporate level, within the institutions of the military, or among the pressure groups who influence legislation and secure their interests through the members of Congress and the Executive Branch. Power, he adds, is allocated through these institutions. They determine and control the agenda of public behavior. This transition was sanctioned before the turn of the century when Justice Stephen A. Field gave a new interpretation to the Fourteenth Amendment. He argued that business corporations were "persons" and should be guaranteed the same rights as individuals. This interpretation of the Amendment to the Constitution took place at a time when social Darwinism was the root metaphor underlying the business ethics of rampant commercialism (Hofstadter, 1944). The corporate mentality is perhaps best characterized by Nelson Aldrich, son-in-law of John D. Rockefeller who argued against the election of Senators in Congress on the basis of geographical distribution. What he favored was a Senate manned officially by representatives from the great business "constituencies" such as steel, coal, copper, railroads, banks, textiles, and so on.

The quest for cultural pluralism in the United States is particularly strong among ethnic minorities who wish to share in the power base of their government. However, the power is based on the needs of an industrial oligarchy (Mills, 1956). As a consequence, what appears to be a governmental sanction of cultural pluralism is really an Anglo assimilation model in disguise. This becomes particularly evident when the distinction between bilingualism and biculturalism is discussed. The former is favored as a transition device leading to the later acquisition of English and the subsequent loss of one's command of a native language. But, biculturalism is contrary to the order society model and constitutes a threat. It is considered un-American and is treated as a disintegrating force leading to social anomie. If cultural pluralism is to become a reality and if the various languages and cultural life styles are to peacefully co-exist in an ecology of humanity, much more is required than mere symbolic victories for minorities under the guise of bilingual education. Instead, instrumental victories are required. Such victories necessitate affirmative legislation on behalf of a pluralistic society and not a disguised front for a version of the anglo-assimilation model.

BILINGUALISM AND THE NATIONAL CURRICULUM

The relationship between the power elite and education becomes clearer when it is seen as a means of serving certain corporate interests. The current system of tracking, testing, and grouping by intellectual and manual skills and abilities serve the needs of channeling of manpower into the market place (Spring, 1976). For the government, the school has become a social-sorting machine. Its role is not to educate, but to socialize one to accept the demands of the commercial world. This use of schooling is not new nor is it unique to the United States. But, what makes the situation in America unique is its commercial use of schooling as a training ground for the urban and rural working classes (Violas, 1978). Unfortunately, teachers and administrators tend to forget this aspect of the foundations of education. They continue to see themselves as being involved in politically neutral tasks. In discussing the establishment of national educational policy since 1945, Joel Spring (1976) gives an in-depth view of the creation of the National Science Foundation and its mandate to meet the needs of science, mathematics, and foreign languages in its battle for supremacy against the Soviet Union. This agency was founded during the era of Sputnik when Americans felt themselves suddenly devalued by the technological accomplishments of their global competitors. If this seems to be an isolated case of the government establishing a national curriculum, others can be readily documented. Arthur Applebee (1974), for example, has show how the teaching of English has varied substantially over the last century and how it has been adjusted toward the needs of the government. At times of war, Applebee notes, the focus is on the value of literture for creating a sense of loyalty to the political culture. Short stories which highlight patriotism is used and minority ethnicity is portrayed in a villainous role (Gossett, 1977). Another use of literature by the government can be found in the teaching of English (St. Clair and Eiseman, 1978a; 1978b). The immigrant is taught English grammar and most teachers of English assume that this is all that they are providing in their instruction. However, the teaching of English to immigrants is essentially a form of political socialization in which a new political culture is advocated and a new perspective on cultural heroes and villains is espoused. In this Americanization curriculum, the members of the elite class were portrayed as heroes and those of the working class and minorities were seen as villains. This use of the English curriculum for socialization is also noted in the work of Louis Kampf and Paul Lauter (1972) who question the belletristic function of literature and see it as a new form of neo-colonialism.

CONCLUDING REMARKS

The language teacher does much more than teach grammar

135

and conduct drills on pronunciation. This person is also an enforcer of social values and a legitimator of political culture. This social and political use of language education may not be seen as a problem for the child who is raised in the dominant culture and shares in its hopes and aspirations, but it is a source of bicultural dissonance for those who are minorities within an order society. This child is usually stigmatized for being different. His or her values are openly questioned by the educational community. The bilingual and bicultural child is treated as an outsider (Becker, 1973) and becomes the victim of verbal and social abuse. The teacher as the enforcer of these official values is at the center of the problem. Such being the case, it would appear that teachers can substantially change the system by moving from a role of social enforcer to civic agent. Unfortunately, the resolution of social problems is never that simple. The teacher has to contend with the administrators of the system. If they devise their own curriculum and if it threatens the status quo they risk the possibility of losing their livelihood. But, even if they are successful as social agents and even if they convince their supervisors and program administrators to join them, the problem still remains. Those higher up on the echelon risk dismissal and public derision. They are all locked within a hierarchy of dependency relationships. The system prevails.

In an order society, it is very difficult to become a social agent without being a part of the power elite. The school teacher in charge of a bilingual curriculum is not in such a position. The values espoused in the classroom fail to enhance the self-concept of the minority child. These exogenous values create more doubt than certainty. They consider all languages and dialects other than standard English as non-entities or as debased forms of speech. They only present one view of history in which the minorities represented in the classroom are portrayed as marginal. In such a social context, differences are categorized in terms of deviancy. In order to overcome these constraints of a closed society, the teacher who had a vested interest in cultural pluralism must assume the role of a social agent. This requires, in part, that the national curriculum be supplemented with educational alternatives; and, it also necessitates involvement in community programs to enlighten those

136

those who are unaware of the advantages that cultural pluralism has for them. However, even though teachers may become social agents in some aspects of their daily instruction, they will always be in a compromising position. They have been employed as social enforcers of the system. Hence, the dilemma persists.

In an order society, education serves the needs of the socio-political system and the classroom teacher assists the school administrator in implementing governmental policies and act as social enforcers of the system. These vertical lines of dependency do not change substantially in a conflict society. What does change is the relative degree of freedom that the school teachers and the administrators have in representing minority interests and concerns. If any noticeable changes do occur with the advent of a conflict society, they come about from modifications in the national curriculum and in the changes of the mainstream culture toward ethnic minorities, their cultures, their forms of linguistic diversity, and their values. It also means that social problems are redefined. The mental illness model of society would no longer be seen as the root metaphor for social action. It would be replaced by a respect for the ecology of life styles which exist within a diverse nation. Tolerance would also come about in the imparting of one's political culture. However, the dilemma of the teacher in a bicultural classroom still remains. It may have been severely attenuated by the lessening demands of the previous order society, but it must now serve new power interests and accommodate to different group interests. A move toward cultural pluralism and toward a conflict society must also mean a concomitant fragmentation of the power structure. A nation that espouses cultural pluralism while maintaining an order society structure controlled by a power elite merely provides symbolic victories for the minorities that they control. It is only when the power base is shared in a conflict society that the vertical dependency relationship of the national curriculum will allow minorities access to the system and it is only in this context that cultural pluralism can serve the needs of the classroom teacher and the school administrator in minority education. Unless these concomitant factors co-occur, the dilemma of the teacher of bicultural education will persist.

REFERENCES

Almond, Gabriel and Verba, Sidney. The Civic Culture. Princeton: Princeton University Press, 1963.

Applebee, Arthur N. Tradition and Reform in the Teaching of English: A History. Urbana, Illinois: National Council of Teachers of English, 1974.

Beard, Charles. An Economic Interpretation of the Constitution of The United States. N.Y.: Macmillian, 1913.

Becker, Howard. Outsiders: Studies in the Sociology of Deviance. N.Y.: Free Press, 1973.

Brown, Phil (Ed.). Radical Psychology. N.Y.: Harper Colophon, 1973.

Brown, Richard H. A Poetic for Sociology: Toward a Logic of Discovery for the Human Sciences. Cambridge, England: Cambridge University Press, 1978.

Dye, Thomas R. and Zeigler, L. Harmon. The Irony of Democracy: An Uncommon Introduction to American Politics. Politics. Belmont, California: Duxbury, A Division of Wadsworth Publishing Co., 1972.

Festinger, Leon. A Theory of Cognitive Dissonance. Palo Alto, California: Stanford University Press, 1957.

Gossett, Thomas F. Race: The History of an Idea in America. N.Y.: Shocken Books, 1977.

Greenbaum, William. American in Search of a New Ideal: An Essay on the Rise of Pluralism. Harvard Educational Review, 1974, 44 (3), 411-440.

Hofstadter, Richard. Social Darwinism in America. Boston, Mass.: Beacon Press, 1944.

Hofstadter, Richard. The Paranoid Style in American Politics and Other Essays. N.Y: Vintage, 1967.

Horton, John. Order and Conflict Theories of Social Problems as Competing Ideologies. American Journal of Sociology, 1966, 71 (May), 701-713.

Jacobson, Wally D. Power and Interpersonal Relations. Belmont, California: Wadsworth Publishing Co., 1972.

Kampf, Louis and Lauter, Paul. The Politics of Literature: Dissenting Essays on the Teaching of English. N.Y.: Vintage Books, 1972.

Kittrie, Nicholas N. The Right to be Different: Deviance and Enforced Therapy. Baltimore, Md.: Penguin Books, 1974.

Klapp, Orrin. Opening and Closing: Strategies of Information Adaptation in Society. Cambridge: Cambridge University Press, 1978.

Lipset, Seymour M. and Raab, Earl. The Politics of Unreason: Right-Wing Extremism in America, 1970-1977. Chicago: University of Chicago Press, 1978.

Lyman, Stanford and Scott, Marvin. A Sociology of the Absurd. Pacific Palisades, California: Goodyear Publishing Co., Inc., 1970.

Mills, C. Wright. The Power Elite. Oxford: Oxford University Press, 1956.

Mueller, Claus. The Politics of Communication: A Study in the Political Sociology of Language, Socialization, and Legitimation. Oxford: Oxford University Press, 1976.

Parenti, Michael. Democracy for the Few. N.Y.: St. Martin's Press, 1974.

Ramirez, Manuel, III and Castañeda, Alfredo. Cultural Democracy, Bicognitive Development, and Education. N.Y.: Academic Press, 1974.

St. Clair, Robert N. The Politics of Language. Word, 1979, 29 (2), 40-67.

St. Clair, Robert N. and Eiseman, James. Language Planning as Political Sociolization. Paper presented at the Mid-America Linguistics Conference, University of Oklahoma, 1978a.

St. Clair, Robert N. and Eiseman, James. The Politics of Teaching English as a Foreign Language. Paper presented at the IXth World Congress of Sociology, Uppsala, Sweden, 1978b.

Schacht, Richard. Alienation. N.Y.: Doubleday, 1970.

Scheff, Thomas J. Being Mentally Ill: A Sociological Theory. Chicago: Aldine Publishing Co., 1967.

Spring, Joel. The Sorting Machine: National Educational Policy Since 1945. N.Y.: David McKay, 1976.

Szasz, Thomas S. The Manufacture of Madness. N.Y.: Dell Publishing Company, 1979.

Violas, Paul. The Training of the Urban Working Class: A History of Twentieth Century of American Education. Chicago: Rand McNally, 1978.

CHAPTER 9

LANGUAGE VARIATION AND BILINGUAL EDUCATION

Fritz Hensey
University of Texas at Austin

A recent Texas Education Agency publication devotes a section to second-language teaching techniques which may be helpful to teachers taking part in bilingual-bicultural education programs. There is a discussion of language development in the child and a display of drills and exercises of the type commonly found in FL textbooks. While the authors recognize that the teacher can expect a great deal of variation in the learners' competence and performance, the emphasis is on developing proficiency in formal Spanish or English.[1]

It is clear that the bilingual's command of Spanish varies widely, particularly on social and regional bases. In many cases, particularly in El Paso and in South Texas, the students' fluency is often such that performance factors come to the foreground. If we assume that one of the goals of a maintenance-oriented program is to broaden students' usage of their vernacular, variation in their written and spoken language acquires major importance.

For some time, the dominant philosophy in second-language teaching has been a behavioristic one, in which language is seen as a patterned set of habits and language teaching as a form of behavior modification in a desired direction. A certain tendency to emphasize rote behavior and to discourage individual creativity reflects the belief that there is a well-defined norm toward which learners should strive. An utterance may be "correct" or "deviant" with respect to the norm. There is a great concern with negative transfer or "interference" between the language being learned and some other language(s). Where standardization is desirable, most variation is likely to suspect either as being deviant or as creating unnecessary complications in teaching, difficulty in evaluation, or imprecision in description.

141

SOCIAL AND EDUCATIONAL ISSUES

Another philosophy of language and language learning which is increasingly challenging the so-called behaviorist or empiricist approach is that which some writers are calling rationalist.   In some ways a return to earlier philosophies of language, this approach sees language as an innate prosperity of human beings which is acquired as part of the maturation process and which manifests itself as rule-governed behavior.   The descriptive model tends to be some form of generative/transformational grammar, at least in some of the generativists' assumptions if not in the precise form that those grammarians use to describe languages.   Two such assumptions are the distinction between abstract competence and observable performance, and the notion of a grammar as a specification of how the user of language relates deep or conceptual structure to those surface which express or manifest deep structure.[2]

Some sociolinguists concern themselves with linguistics variables, alternate ways of realizing particular underlying structures.   Two sentences may be synonymous to some extent..e.g., English "Who(m) were you speaking to?/To whom were you speaking", Spanish "Lo conozco/le conozco"...but the fact that one occurs rather than the other(s) is quite meaningful.   Variables may be phonological, lexical, morphosyntactic; they may be determined by the user's background, his intention, circumstances of utterance, etc. While language variation as such is very commonly observed, often to the point of banality, FL texts usually fail to define major variations in usage in a pedagogically useful way.   Here, the treatment of variation by the sociolinguist may have something to contribute, particularly to those interested in second- or native-language instruction for bilinguals.[3]

Consider phonological variation.   One trait of American English which is socially meaningful involves the treatment of words written with r in syllable-final position: hard, partner, arm, etc.   One speaks of "r-less dialects", i.e. those in which the r is "dropped" or "replaced" by schwa or "compensated for" by vowel lengthening.   Non-r-less dialects articulate the r as a non-lateral liquid (for many speakers, a retroflex).   There is another and more precise way to describe this phenomen.

142

Assuming that there is some level of phonology more abstract, "higher up", than that of actual pronunciation, we may claim that words like hard, partner, etc., contain an /r/ for all speakers and hearers. How that /r/ actually occurs (including whether it occurs at all) can be stated by rules whose conditioning may be stylistic, grammatical, regional, and so forth. The underlying /r/, according to such a rule, would be pronounced in n̲ different ways (including not at all). Each of the n̲ ways would be a variant, and each variant would be predictable (with some degree of confidence) once the conditioning factors are known. All this is from the point of view of the speaker, but the rule is merely reversed for the hearer: the hearer interprets a certain segment as representing an underlying /r/, and at the same time he may make some assumption about the speaker or the context of the utterance based on his assessment of the conditioning of the variant used.

In Spanish, there is a phonological variable relating to the pronunciation of /e/ before a vowel, in forms like pasear, león, etc. If /e/ is unstressed and the following vowel is stressed, e/e may occur as a syllabic mid vowel (leon) or as a non-syllabic, somewhat higher vowel (león) or (lión). The popular perception of this is reflected in spellings like pasiar, lión, used inter alia in comic strips to mark colloquial or substandard speech.

For the latter variable, which we may define as "articulation of unstressed /e/ directly followed by a stressed vowel", there are at least two major variants: (1) articulation as (e) and (2) articulation as non-syllabic (e) or (i). The first variant is usually considered standard, the second informal, colloquial, and sometimes substandard. As an example of misinterpretation of a variant, consider the form sarampión. Some speakers hypercorrect to sarampeón; i.e., they assume that the surface (i) represents underlying /e/ rather than /i/, as in the case.

Similar formulations can be made in vocabulary. Words or expressions which are basically synonymous...e.g., English sets like (state/postulate/calm...), (addict/head...) or Spanish ones like (dentista/odontologo...), (persona/bato/-tipo/fulano/individuo...)...are seen to alternate according to such criteria as stylistic intention; such variables are commonly called "technical", "slang", "informal", etc., which is equivalent to setting up conditions for the choice of a particular variant.

Finally, we can find variation in the rules of grammar which produce different but somehow synonymous sentence patterns, inflectional processes, and the like. In English, for instance, the complementizer <u>that</u> may or may not appear in certain constructions: I think (doubt, etc.) (that) it's possible. It's presence or absence is not a matter of chance but reflects such conditions as style and sentence rhythm.

In Spanish, loísta dialects are those in which the direct object clitic pronoun used with certain verbs (e.g., conocer, ver, amar...) is <u>le</u> (fem. la), whereas leísta dialects use <u>le</u> in these cases. Another way to state this is to say that, assuming <u>le</u> always manifests the accusative and <u>le</u> the dative, certain verbs use either dative or accusative when a clitic pronoun is chosen. It is not clear whether the conditioning is regional, stylistic, lexically conditioned, or a combination of these criteria.

In setting up the description of a variable, one must decide what the underlying structure is. Where lexicon is concerned, it may be useful to ask how many ways a certain concept can be expressed by the learner in speech or in writing. Another form of the same question is to ask how many variants is the reader or listener likely to encounter. One typical Latin American lexical variable is the generic term for beans: <u>frijoles, habichuelas, poroto,</u> are three such variants. Their conditioning appears to be regional. A given person will tend to have an active command of at least one of them; his passive control of the others will depend on the range of his experience.

A bilingual's language variation includes not only sets of variables within each language but the possibility of using either or both of his languages. Consider how he might express the concept "to wax (a floor, a car, etc.)". One possibility is that he lacks a term in one language but has it in the other: <u>waxear</u> is often heard in lieu of a standard form like <u>encerar.</u> The latter may or may not exist in the bilingual's passive vocabulary, or it may exist in a referentially or stylistically different sense. The point here is that for some bilinguals, a set of alternate expressions need not all be in the same languages; the very fact that ideally "balanced" bilinguals are quite rare in our milieu strongly suggests that this process is quite common.

Another form of variation often found among bilinguals in this area is the use of non-standard (regional, archaic) forms in lieu of those which the school system would like to foster. The concept "brakes" may be manifested as (manea, freno, brecas, Eng. brakes); this includes standard, regional Anglicism, and code-switching variants).

Phonological variants typical among bilinguals show at least two forms: those apparently due to interference of one of their languages in question and which become problems when they are judged excessively regional or substandard. An example of the first concerns the English used by many Spanish-English bilinguals. For native monolinguals, there appears to be a rule in English which states that when word-final /s/ stands for a morpheme (ie.e., a plural marker or a very ending) it is pronounced voices [/z/] following a voiced consonant or a vowel. Forms like sees, legs, falls, following this rule are pronounced with final /z/. Many bilingual, however, fail to apply this rule...they will pronounce such forms with voiceless /s/. Further, the bilingual may apply a different rule, one appropriate to Spanish, which states that final /s/ is pronounced voiced when it is followed by a voiced consonant. Thus, sees him is pronounced [sisxm] but sees me as [sizmi]. The latter pronounciation would be felt as "right" by the native English speaker, but it is right for the wrong reason: the /s/ of sees is being voiced because of the following /m/ and not because of the preceding vowel. The first case, sees him with voiceless /s/, is "wrong" by the English rule but "right" by the Spanish rule. The speaker "has an accent".

In the Spanish of many Chicanos, the segment written ll (as in silla, milla, ella...) appears to disappear in such forms, giving what one might write sia, mia, ea. To state this more precisely, we may say the following: there is a phoneme /L/ which may be pronounced in several ways. Leaving aside the forms that it takes in other parts of the world- ...e.g.. [L] in Peru and Bolivia, [ẑ] or [ŝ] in Argentina and Uruguay...we find that it is pronounced as a more or less constricted alveopalatal, which we can represent as [y].

The less constricted this sound is, the more it ends to a y-glide or yod. When it follows a front vowel, particularly /i/, this yod may be absorbed by the syllabic. Thus míLa/, [éLa] (milla, ella), come out as [miya], [mia] and [eya], [eía], [eá].

Here are two examples of grammatical or morphosyntactic variation found among bilinguals in the Southwest. At the level of the sentence, both English and Spanish have construction which have a sentential complement following verbs of the type want/querer, prefer/preferir, like/ gustar, etc. Sentences like I want to go/quiero ir have been analyzed to show a structure of the sort I want (I-to-go) and Quiero (yo-ir), where the parenthesized subordinate clause will end up in the infinitive, subjunctive, gerund, etc., according to the type of very occuring in the main sentence as well as certain syntactic conditions.

Want and querer are only partially alike: "I want to go" and "Quiero ir", manifesting the above structures, show similar patterning, but cf. "Quiero que vayas" and "I want for you to go."

Other English/Spanish pair of sentential verbs differ more sharply, e.g. I like do/doing that vs. Me gusta hacerlo (but not: *haciéndolo). In writing Spanish, many Chicano use a gerund following the English rule rather than an infinitive as standard Spanish requires: me gusta leyendo historias, prefiero viajando en avión, etc. Here, we may formalize this by saying that the bilingual classifies verbs like gustar, preferir as using either infinitive (me gusta ir), subjunctive (prefiero que vayas), or gerund (me gusta/prefiero yendo). The latter variant may be associated with written Spanish; in writing, of course, the learner will normally use English in the US public school system. The third variant, with the gerund, is "incorrect" according to the norm followed by most monolingual Spanish speakers. By formalizing it in terms of a variable rule, we may go beyond merely classifying it as a "deviation: or "error". We state clearly what is happening, in a way that can be generalized to other verbs and sentence types; we define the variants which occur; and we attempt to account for the distribution of those variants.

Another grammatical variable not due to interference is alternation in the inflection of certain tenses of particualr verbs. Consider the present subjunctive, 1st person plural, of such verbs as <u>decir, haber,</u> querer... We may set up moderately complex rule which says the following:

The first plural form consists of the subunctive stem formative vowel /a/ plus the ending for 1st plural. That ending is either <u>mos</u> or <u>nos</u>. If it is <u>nos</u>, the theme vowel is stressed, and the forms are <u>díaganos</u>, <u>háyamos</u> (or <u>háiganos</u>) <u>quiéranos</u>. If it is <u>mos</u>, either the theme vowel or the stem vowel is stressed: <u>dígamos</u> or <u>digámos</u>, <u>hayamos</u> or <u>hayámos</u>, etc. Thus, there are two major variants (stress on theme vowel, digámos, or stress on stem vowel; in the latter case, there are two subvariants: <u>dígamos</u> and <u>díganos</u>. A form like <u>haiga(mos)</u> has nothing to do with this particular rule: it represents a different rule, one providing alternate stem forms for certain verbs. There would be still another rule covering forms like <u>vide/o,truje/o,</u> and still another for <u>semos</u> as an alternate to <u>somos.</u>

When a rule for variation has been set up, it will contain (1) the underlying structure in question, (2) the alternate ways in which that structure can occur, (3) the conditions under which each variant is likely to be found, and (4) some assessment of the variable as a learning problem. In the last example, we have a rule which shows that 1st pl present subjunctive can be manifested in three different ways; that the difference involves stress placement and the choice of -<u>mos</u> or <u>nos</u> as the person/number market; it may be seen that forms like <u>diágmos</u>, <u>quéramos</u> are the standard variant, <u>dígamos</u> and <u>quieramos</u> are substandard but may be used by speakers who also have the other variant as a marker of informality, while the <u>díganos</u>, <u>muéranos</u> variant is substandard and rustic.

Defining a particular variable leads to its classification as a learning problem and hence to the type of approach that may be desirable in either the textbook or the classroom situation. The basic dimensions of language are the syntagmatic (horizontal) and the paradigmatic (vertical). If a problem is seen as syntagmatic it is because the emphasis is on such matters as word order, agreement or other cases in which some form of selection or positioning is involved, and the context in which selection occurs is is immediately evident. In Spanish, for instance, gender-number agreement between nouns and their determiners or modifiers is a common syntagmatic matter. A typical variable involving concord is the set of Greek neuters (idioma, sistema, problema, etc.) which for some students are treated as feminine rather than masculine: *la idioma, etc. In English, a problem involving word-order arises in indirect questions: Ask him where he lives alternating with *Ask him where does he live represent two variants of the same transformation, namely the one that joins two sentences to form an indirect question.

Paradigmatic or vertical problems are seen to arise when the emphasis is on selection of a particular form or rule from a set of mutually exclusive possibilities, i.e., from a paradigm. Verb conjugations and other inflections constitute obvious examples from both English and Spanish. A frequent problem of this sort is Spanish is the choice of imperfect or preterite, indicative or subjunctive, in cases where the conditioning factor is outside the sentence itself; e. g. where the choice depends on the speaker or writer's overall intention. With subjunctive, for instance, the fact that the conjunction antes requires the subjunctive in the verb of the subordinate clause (antes de que te vavas) is one of selection in a clearly statable context, hence it is a syntagmatic matter; on the other hand, whether the indicative or subjunctive is used in a relative clause (una persona que me conocía/conociera) is not always dependent on some element present in the sentence itself but rather in user's intention. In this case, often it is a difference between specified/unspecified real/hypothetical, or the like. In English, the so-called "strong" or "irregular" verbs are conjugated according to several different patterns of vowel alternation...e.g., the set (sing, swim...) is distinct form the set (set, hit...)...and there appears to be no external clue, such as the physical appearance of the verb stem or its meaning, to help the user predict just what pattern is to be used. Students' difficulties with paradigmatic matters should be seen not merely as "errors" but as instances of variable rules which can be clearly stated. The difficulty consists of using a variant which needs to be replaced by a different, "correct" variant.

148

In an approach to language teaching based on pattern
drills, syntagmatic problems are usually approached by
"transformation" drills and paradigmatic ones by "substitution". It is possible that other drill types...expansion,
replacement, rejoinder, and the like...may be grouped with
one or the other of the main drill types which one may call
syntagmatic drills and paradigmatic drills. Even the sort of
exercise that calls for the learner to answer questions
(Where do you live? I live in, etc.) may be seen as problems
in selection whose conditioning is given by the trigger sentence: an erroneous response to the above world would be
(Where do you live? *Your name is John.)

An exercise that may be useful for students in composition courses is the following. Assume that there is a
problem variable consisting of whether to use ser or estar.
This problem is very real for some Chicanos as well as for
non-native students of Spanish. If we limit ourselves to
those cases where the choice of verb is conditioned by the
sentence context, we can state for instance that estar is
selected by the present participle, ser by the presence of a
noun phrase predicate (NP __ NP), and so forth. Most cases,
however, require some judgement as to what the deep structure
is; for example, given a past participle ser marks a true
passive (fue pintado) while estar has a stative meaning (está
pintado). Rather than attempting to classify these many different processes in terms of what drills could be used to
reinforce desire usage, the students themselves will make the
analysis.

Students are asked to select from their reading (including transcriptions of originally spoken material) a given
number of examples of use of each verb, ser and estar, complete with the immediate context in which it is used. They
are furnished a listing, which they will have helped to draw
up, of various reasons why the writer or speaker selected one
verb rather than the other. This assumes that the variables
consists of using either ser or estar, as determined by
several clearly defined criteria.

The students are then asked to decide why each particular choice was made in terms of the listing. Most cases
are self-evident, but some will require discussion and study
by the learner.

In another application of this approach, students are asked to go over their own work in terms of a particular learning problem that merits attention. Exercises of this nature, which are done outside the class, are done in a spirit of restoring to the student some of the responsibility for his own learning which an overly mechanical application of mimicry-and-memorization.

The variable-approach outlined above is basically diagnostic. It suggests that language variation can be seen as rule-governed behavior, such that there are certain underlying structures (in grammar, phonology, and lexicon) to which rules will apply. There are two or more variants, each of which is partly predictable. Sometimes the problem is to increase the number of variants, as when the bilingual's stylistic range is very limited or where he has to fall back on the second language to express something. In other cases, a particular variant may be inappropriate and the hope is to replace it with a more appropriate one.

The approach is descriptive rather than prescriptive. It sees bilingual education as a device for increasing the student's options rather than by replacing one set of possibilities by another set. It considers variation in the bilingual's language background and performance as somethings that can be put to use to help him become a more effective speaker and writer.

NOTES

1. Texas Education Agency: A Resource Manual for Implementing Bilingual Education Programs (Regional Educational Agencies Project on International Education). Austin, 1975.

2. For a brief description of these trends, see Conrad Diller: Generative Grammar, Structural Linguistic, and Language Teaching. Rowley, Mass: Newbury House, 1971.

3. For a discussion of some of the variables appearing in corpus material gathered at El Paso, see F. Hensey, "Grammatical Variables in Southwestern U.S. Spanish": in Linguistics 108. 5-27 (1973). For a different discussion, which includes phonological traits, see Rosaura Sanchez, "Nuestra circunstancia linguistica" in El Grito 6.45-74, 1972.

SOCIAL AND EDUCATIONAL ISSUES

BIBLIOGRAPHY

Fishman, Joshua A.   1974. A Sociology of Bilingual Educa-
     ation, OECO-73-05882, U.S. Office of Education (ms.).

Hargadon, Fred. 1975. "It May Be Harder to Get Top Stu-
     dents", Stanford Observer, 4, (February).

Panshin, Alexei. 1968. Heinlein in Dimension: A Critical
     Analysis, Chicago: Advent Publishers.

Shopen, Timothy. 1974. "Linguistics For Non-Majors", paper
     read at a workshop at the XXVth Annual Round Table,
     Georgetown University, Washington, D.C.

CHAPTER 10

CLASSROOM VARIABLES IN SUCCESSFUL

BILINGUAL/BICULTURAL EDUCATION

Lilith M. Haynes
New Mexico State University

INTRODUCTION

Social and linguistic variation exist in all classrooms, whether they are in monolingual, bilingual, or multilingual societies; the specific concerns of the teacher and student operating in a bilingual society, however, are those with which the questions of social and linguistic variation are considered in this paper. The bilingual/bicultural classroom might be ideally construed as one in which two languages are used for the instruction of any of the subjects in the curriculum, and not a classroom in which the use of more than one language is confined to the teaching of one of those languages, whether in attempts to erase or compensate for the knowledge of one of those lanugages by the students. In the ideal bilingual classroom, the students are simultaneously introduced to the values and norms of the two societies which generate the languages used for instruction, as well. There are places in the world where this ideal is pursued, and in several of these places the ideal is pursued, and in several of these places the ideal is also achieved. Fishman's recent study (1974 ms.) of bilingual education programs throughout the world has found a .89 correlation between three sociolinguistic factors and absolute success of these programs as reported by the people responsible for these programs. As we note the proliferation of conferences and symposia to define the rationes and techniques for bilingual/bicultural programs in the United States, many years after the allocation of substantial fiscal and human resources, we find that few, if any, local programs either pursue the ideal or report measures of consistent success when the ideal is pursued. In this paper, I underscore variables informing the factors defined as vital to successful bilingual/bicultural education, and consider some variables which are adherent to them; special reference is made to the situation as I have been able to observe it in the United States.[1]

SOCIAL AND EDUCATIONAL ISSUES

Variable List

MACRO-SOCIETAL FACTORS

1.   Ascription of value to the knowledge of the marked language (i.e. the language not normally used for instruction) by all members of the society.

2.   Ascription of elite dominance to the unmarked language (i.e. the language normally used for instruction) by all members of the society.

3.   Acknowledgement of positive economic and international functions for the unmarked language by the whole society.

TEACHER VARIABLES

4. Knowledge and use of both languages by all teachers in consistent accordance with grammatical norms.

5.   Thorough and current knowledge of subjects, including language, by teachers.

6.   Use of both languages present in a society for the instruction of all subjects in a curriculum.

TEACHER-STUDENT VARIABLES

7.   Familiarity with student variation on the part of teachers.

8.   Acceptance of student viewpoints by teachers.

9. Thorough and consistent correction of student errors by teachers.

DISCUSSION

MACRO-SOCIETAL FACTORS

Factor 1 would be realized if all members of a speech-community were given to positive societal validity to knowledge of what are usually called "minority lanugages", the languages natives to some--and some cases most--members of that speech-community. Thus, in a community in which some members speak Armenian and other members speak English, both Armenian and English would be treated as vital to the definition of the particular nature of that community and to its daily interactions; all members of the community would know both Armenian and English so that they could participate in the various domains of social interaction shared by members of the community. In the same manner, in a community such as the Southwest USA, knowledge of the languages present in the community-native American languages and dialects; Spanish; English and its dialects of the Ranch, the ghetto, the Seminolé community; Tex-Mex, Romanés, Armenian would be seen as valuable to all members of the community.

It is interesting that in the discussion of Factors 2 and 3, few objections are ever raised: everyone can understand that English is the language of elite dominance, and see why it should continue to be thus treated: similarly, the economic and international functions of English are acknowledged by most people to be entirely positive. The success of bilingual/bicultural programs hinges, nonetheless, upon all three factors, and so the first factor must be generated in those societies in which it is not present, and encouraged to survive in those societies where it is emerging.

In a society as fissured and institutionally racist as the United States, a number of objections are usually raised when professional analysts of the sociology of language try to suggest introduction of the first factor; such objections are a) that learning more than one language interferes with the learning of other, more important skills; b) that teachers do not have enough time to teach more than one language; c) that teaching non-elite languages interferes with learning

155

of the elite language, which is the only useful language in a
society.

It has been widely observed and documented that language
learning skills seem innate to all human beings -since only
humans learn to use languages in a dynamic fashion, and since
all humans not severely handicapped by brain damage learn at
least one language.   In those situations where social interaction has not been possible with the use of one language,
new languages have been generated or learned; in multilingual
countries such as Switzerland, all members of the society
learn all of the languages of the society, and there is great
social cohesion. These instances of bi- and multi-lingualism
involved at their inception the will, effort, and practice
necessary for the acquisition of any human skill.   Although
aptitude is seen to vary among individuals, it is possible
for any normal human being to learn to jog, to drive a car,
or even to be a racist, should the opportunities for learning
be present.   Once any of these skills is acquired, it is
generalizable to new situations, and so the city dweller who
leaners to jog in smog can also learn to jog in the rare aire
of the desert; the driver of a Ford pick-up truck can learn
to maneuver a Maserati; and so the Peoria racist can transfer the habits of racism to Las Cruces or South Boston.
Similarly, with will, effort, and practice, the person who
learns a language--and all human beings do--can generalize
the knowledge of grammatical organization of the native language to new language-learning situations. In all of these
eventualities, adaptations have to be made, and to the extent
that they are not made by humans, the activity involved is
that of the cat which, having sat on a hot stove, will never
sit on another stove, whether it is hot or cold; such
activity is inhuman and animal.   Few people suggest that
learning a variety of physical skills is injurious to physical fitness; the generalization of this attitude to the
acquisition of intellectual skills would certainly enhance
the success of bilingual/bicultural education programs, and
the social health of the communities in which they are attempted.   The allocation of time and resources for learning
and teaching is dictated by the wish for that teaching and
learning; the allocation of so many minutes, hours, days,
weeks, months, years, for the teaching in language X or language Y is essentially a function of the wish to do.   Moreover, it becomes less important for administrators to compute

156

intricate allocations when everyone in the learning
situation--teacher and student and community--accepts as valuable to to the whole society all the learning that is to
take place, for then it becomes simple to move from one to
another language in a democratic manner. Upon scientific observation of the facts, it is apparent that the elite language is useful only in certain areas of social interaction,
viz. those areas where elite standards of etiquette are appropriate. The elite member of society, finding him- or herself in a non-elite situation, may survive only through
knowledge of the non-elite language. Moreover, the formal
styles of the elite language, which ideally are those taught
in the classroom, do not provide even the elite member of
society with the total repertoire necessary for elite social
interactions; the non-elite members of society need to learn
these formal styles, but they, and the elite members of
society, need to learn the informal and other intermediate
styles as well.

TEACHER VARIABLES

Actual oral and written grammatical use of language--
which provides a model for students--would be expected in a
successful teaching situation, and it would involve fluent
transitions among the various codes and styles in accordance
with the norms defined by the speakers of the language; it
would be formal in formal situations, and informal in informal situations, and never incorrect. Unfortunately, as
perusal of teachers' corrections on students' written work or
careful listening to teachers' oral language behavior would
indicate, it cannot be assumed--even when they are consciously attempting to be formal users of the elite
language--that teachers are fluent users of the elite language. Teachers who know only one of the languages present
in a bilingual society, and this imperfectly, are serious
handicaps to the success of education, and especially
bilingual/bicultural educaton.

English, the elite language, is widely used to teach
other languages in many bilingual programs; rarely is the
converse true, however, partly because of a lack of imagina-
tion, partly because of a lack of knowledge of the other language, and partly because the other language is not treated
as language. The second of these reasons is perhaps the most
difficult to deal with, but when teachers are required to be

157

able to reach English via another language, a precise knowledge of English, and a fluent knowledge of the other language
will also be required of language teachers. Teachers who do
not possess or maintain thorough, current knowledge of their
subjects are in the double jeopardy of transmitting inaccurate information and of being detected very quickly and
punished in a number of ways by their students. Language
teachers need perhaps to be more careful than other teachers
in meeting the criteria of preparation, because they are
charged with providing the tools whereby other subjects in
the curriculum can be learned. In order to deal with lin-
gusitics variation in their classrooms, language teachers
need to know their languages enough to speak and write them,
and they need precise scientific knowledge of the nature and
history of the languages, so that they can recognize the pro-
cessual, changing nature of language, the idiolectal and
dialectal variation expressed by students, and the causation
of the errors which students make.

But the success of bilingual/bicultural education is not
measured by the ability of students to use two languages in
language classes; rather, success is measured by the ability
of students to perform in all situations of social interaction by means of two languages. One requirement for the
production of such students is the training of students in
two languages in many subjects, so that a requirement for all
teachers would seem to be the ability to teach their subject
in two languages. It is very likely that when the pressure
is taken off language classes in bilingual education programs, language learning--of the other language as well as
the elite language--will take place.

TEACHER-STUDENT VARIABLES

The literature on foreign-language learning indicates
that this learning is most successful when teachers as well
as students are interested in the non-material, integrative
rewards of language learning and the material, instrumental
rewards of fluent language use. Teachers who know and like
the languages they do not normally speak, and which their
charges do normally speak, are in a position to like their
students enough to be able to teach them. The teaching of
anything is, in the final analysis, the teaching of people by
people, so that it is helpful to the teaching if the people
doing the teaching also have the advantage of concentrating

on the teaching instead of concentrating on disliking the people being taught. Affection is a function of familiarity, so that teachers who wish to be successfully integrative in their teaching need to be reasonably familiar with the people they teach. The names and physiognomic characteristics of students are frequently imprecise indicators of actual social identity: the Spanish-surnamed student may be, or may feel, Native American - and vice versa; the Native-American-looking student may be Black; the "Black" student may be Mexican-American, and so forth. In addition to looking beyond the surface characteristics of students and the stereotypes generated by former societal pressures, teachers need to be aware of the reflexes of ethnic and social variation present in their classrooms and provide the climate in which they can find expression. I had to be told, for example, by one of my world-wise Apache students that it was extremely annoying to my Navajo--and especially my male Navajo--students to be singled out in the classroom, even for praise; I had to learn from a teaching assistant that <u>chicanas</u> like to be left to sit quietly at the back of the room, especially in their freshman year. Until I knew these things, my establishment strategies of "class-participation" and "eye-contact" were tuning out my explanations about syntax and theme-structure for those students to whom they did not apply culturally. Other variants of differentiation among students to which teachers need to pay attention are poverty--which can disallow the purchase of cassette recorders by some students of teachers who think it terribly innovative to grade on cassette tapes, for example; illness, including mental illness, which is currently reported at a level of ten percent in the American population, and at somewhat higher levels in certain areas of the country--which suggests that of every thirty students in a classroom three or more may need special handling; and other reflexes of social organizaton, such as hunger and claustrophobia--which make it difficult for students to perform during their lunch hours or in dismal, over-heated classroom. It is possible to move classes outdoors or to other times in the day, to set material requirements for classes at levels reachable by all students, and to acquire elementary counseling skills in order to provide learning environments for all persons in bilingual/bicultural classrooms, but many teachers balk at requesting their administrations to be human enough to do these things, and force themselves and their students to ensure lack of success for their programs.

159

The teacher who visits a "beauty-operator" every week is a member of a societal sector different from the student who appears in very short cut-offs, cornrows, and a bushy beard, but this societal variation is not inherently bad. However, when this teacher invalidates the personality and creative activity of this student, and punishes the student for membership in another societal sector, while rewarding even incomplete mimicking of the teacher's criteria for social expression, social variation in the classroom becomes unlawful; sadly, this eventuality is rampant. As Fred Hargadon, the Dean of Admissions at Standford has pointed out:

> "The most glaring example of the goals of diversity being unfulfilled is the relatively high degree of separateness which characterizes the way in which minority students, on the one hand, and non-minority students, on the other hand, go through Stanford these days.

Teachers need instead to create environments in which all voices will have their place, whatever they say. In this connection, Timothy Shopen's comments are illustrative:

> "Teachers and their students are unequal in their knowledge...but an interesting observation from a student is worth just as much as one from a teacher; teachers sometimes try to create a situation where they appear to know all the answers. This is damaging to education always and especially with students to think of themselves as outside."

Teachers who can bear to criticized, who can do the assignments which students are set and read these assignments aloud just like everyone else in the classroom create the type of classroom situation in which variation is welcome. In this type of classroom, there is not anarchy, but learning; as one of my students noted, the function of the teacher is to ensure that order is maintained:

> "...would stop writing if there was no
> one to read their writing. () In an
> English class if there wasn't an audience
> (the teacher), the student could write
> anything and get away with it."

In a classroom where variation is valid, sharing is encouraged. Teachers do not have the right to demand that students exteriorize those facets of their personalities which they wish to keep private; neither do they have the right to define the subjects and opinions which will be acceptable. These facts raise the questions of what will be shared; what the student enjoys; what the student wishes or needs to know more about, from whom, and when. The answers to these questions can be given only by the student, and the teacher who is secure enough to ask these questions, needs to be ready to respond to a variety of responses from students. If teachers are to be responsible for the education of students, they need first to be fully aware of the educational apparatus which each student brings into the classroom situation. The educational experiences of students may include things of which teachers are ignorant, as well as the things teachers desire to teach, so that sharing of needs and goals at the outset can not only ensure that education will take place, but that efforts will be directed only toward education. In the bilingual/bicultural classroom the nature of education is conceivably a permutation of the various needs articulated. It is important for teachers to operate on the premise that students do wish to learn, for this is the factor which determines whether a student will attend school or be truant. More particularly in bilingual/bicultural classrooms, it is important to operate on the premise that all students wish to know about each other; the "minority" student wants to know what makes the non-minority student tick, and vice versa, as one of my non-minority students indicates:

> "During the course I received a look at
> ideas from some minority groups' point of
> view: for example the girl in the Watts
> area and the conditions that ruled her
> life, the cigar salesman who had given up
> a happy life to come to the land of
> opportunity, the Shamanistic beliefs of
> the Indians, and the Chicano and

161

> Pachuco poetry. It isn't that I neces-
> sarily understand their way of seeing
> things, but I had never stopped to think
> of them in such a light before: these
> are other effects that I received from
> this class which are probably just per-
> sonal, but I do want to share them...the
> fact that I was allowed to write about my
> faith uncriticized () add up to quite an
> experience and I appreciate it."

In a buddy system, students can learn from each other; and in groups, they can look outside the classroom at other types of social organization, how these features affect them and their families and friends, and, in turn, develop strategies for dealing with these features - which is education.

The final variable deals with the thorough and consistent correction of student errors: when all of a student's errors are not indicated, the student has every right to believe that his or her performance is as good as the teacher indicates, and to object when the grade is not consistent with the level of performance indicated, or to be confused when the same or other teachers punish or point out as errors such things as those the teacher has not marked wrong. It is old-fashioned, perhaps, and certainly time-consuming to correct student errors, but it is damaging to students to see their work bathed in corrections, the answer comes clearly from the students: they do not wish to "get away with anything". Moreover, students can recognize progress when the number of corrections diminishes as the semester or quarter progresses. As noted above, the acquisition of skills involves, apart from the will to learn, effort, and practice: students who are required to correct their mistakes will learn the correct skills, and teachers who provide all of the humanistic support indicated above will find that students do not object to correcting their mistakes.

CONCLUSIONS

The concern of this paper has been to pose some new

challenges in old dimensions; as Alexei Panshin has pointed out, "the unfamiliar seen against the unfamiliar is all too apt to seem chaotic or irrelevant; the familiar seen with the familiar is...merely familiar, the same thing seen for the thousandth time; but the familiar seen with the unfamiliar illuminates." In all three sections of the discussion I trust that some illumination has been achieved, so that bilingual/bicultural education, in paying attention to the variables operating outside and inside classrooms, can be increasingly successful.

NOTE

[1]My observations are based on teaching writing to "disadvantaged" students over the past three academic years; I am indebted to my students and teaching assistant for many of the insights presented here.